EASY ITALIAN
COOKERY

EASY ITALIAN COOKERY

Grange
BOOKS

Published by Grange Books
An imprint of Books & Toys Limited
The Grange
Grange Yard
London SE1 3AG
By arrangement with Ebury Press

ISBN 1 85627 176 5

Consultant editor: Jeni Wright
Editors: Veronica Sperling and Barbara Croxford
Design: Mike Leaman
Illustrations: John Woodcock and Kate Simunek
Photography: David Johnson
Cookery: Susanna Tee, Maxine Clark, Janet Smith

Filmset by Advanced Filmsetters (Glasgow) Ltd

Printed and bound in Italy by
New Interlitho, S.p.a., Milan

CONTENTS

COOKERY NOTES

Follow either metric or imperial measures for the recipes in this book as they are not inter-changeable. Sets of spoon measures are available in both metric and imperial size to give accurate measurement of small quantities. All spoon measures are level unless otherwise stated. When measuring milk we have used the exact conversion of 568 ml (1 pint).

* Size 4 eggs should be used except when otherwise stated.

† Granulated sugar is used un-less otherwise stated.

OVEN TEMPERATURE CHART

°C	°F	Gas mark
110	225	$\frac{1}{4}$
130	250	$\frac{1}{2}$
140	275	1
150	300	2
170	325	3
180	350	4
190	375	5
200	400	6
220	425	7
230	450	8
240	475	9

KEY TO SYMBOLS

1.00* Indicates minimum preparation and cooking times in hours and minutes. They do not include prepared items in the list of ingredients; calcu-lated times apply only to the method. An asterisk * indicates extra time should be allowed, so check the note below symbols.

⊟ Chef's hats indicate degree of difficulty of a recipe: no hat means it is straightforward; one hat slightly more complicated; two hats indicates that it is for more advanced cooks.

£ Indicates a recipe which is good value for money; £ £ indicates an expensive recipe. No £ sign indicates an inexpensive recipe.

✳ Indicates that a recipe will freeze. If there is no symbol, the recipe is unsuitable for freezing. An asterisk * indicates special freezer instructions so check the note immediately below the symbols.

309 cals Indicates calories per serving, including any sugges-tions (e.g. cream, to serve) given in the ingredients.

METRIC CONVERSION SCALE

	LIQUID			SOLID	
Imperial	Exact conversion	Recommended ml	Imperial	Exact conversion	Recommended g
$\frac{1}{4}$ pint	142 ml	150 ml	1 oz	28.35 g	25 g
$\frac{1}{2}$ pint	284 ml	300 ml	2 oz	56.7 g	50 g
1 pint	568 ml	600 ml	4 oz	113.4 g	100 g
$1\frac{1}{2}$ pints	851 ml	900 ml	8 oz	226.8 g	225 g
$1\frac{3}{4}$ pints	992 ml	1 litre	12 oz	340.2 g	350 g
For quantities of $1\frac{3}{4}$ pints and over, litres and fractions of a litre have been used.			14 oz	397.0 g	400 g
			16 oz (1 lb)	453.6 g	450 g
			1 kilogram (kg) equals 2.2 lb.		

EASY ITALIAN COOKERY

The essence—and beauty—of Italian cookery lies in its simplicity, so you need have no fear about tackling any of the recipes in this book. Quick to make and fun to do, they're all so delicious that your only problem will be in choosing where to start.

Every occasion is catered for in the recipe section, which has the added bonus of a colour photograph for every dish, plus step-by-step illustrations to help with cooking methods. There are Soups & Starters for dinner parties, plus Main Courses, Vegetables and Desserts. Then there are special chapters for snacks and impromptu meals—Pasta, Rice & Gnocchi, Pizzas, Cheese & Eggs, and Salads.

The section called Useful Information and Basic Recipes at the end of the book is packed with back-up information. Specialist ingredients; how to use them, where to get them and what to do if they're difficult to obtain; special cooking skills like making pasta, pizza and ice cream; kitchen equipment to make preparation easier and help achieve a more authentic flavour; plus a section containing lots of extra recipes for basic reference—you'll find yourself turning to it time and time again.

Soups and Starters

For everyday, family
meals, the starter or antipasto is usually very
light—maybe a slice or
two of salami, some olives
or anchovies, or a salad or
cold vegetable tossed in a
flavoursome dressing.
The recipes in this
chapter offer inspiration
for more elaborate
starters, the kind an
Italian cook would
prepare for a special
occasion or when enter-
taining guests. Soups fall
into two categories: the
clear and light type
(*brodo*) is usually served
as a first course (*primo
piatto*), whereas the more
substantial soup (*minestra*
or *zuppa*) is served as a
meal in itself.

MINESTRONE
(MIXED VEGETABLE AND PASTA SOUP)

2.30* £ ✳ 332 cals

* plus overnight soaking

Serves 8

50 g (2 oz) butter

50 g (2 oz) pancetta (see page 133)
  or unsmoked streaky bacon,
  rinded and finely chopped

3 onions, skinned and sliced

1 garlic clove, skinned and crushed

2 carrots, peeled and diced

2 sticks celery, washed and diced

225 g (8 oz) dried haricot beans,
  soaked in cold water overnight,
  drained and rinsed

350 g (12 oz) fresh tomatoes,
  skinned and roughly chopped,
  or 226 g (8 oz) can tomatoes with
  their juice

2.3 litres (4 pints) beef stock (see
  page 148)

100 g (4 oz) shelled fresh or frozen
  peas

350 g (12 oz) potatoes, peeled and
  diced

175 g (6 oz) short cut macaroni or
  small pasta shapes

175 g (6 oz) French beans, topped,
  tailed and sliced

225 g (8 oz) cabbage, shredded

15 ml (1 tbsp) chopped fresh
  parsley

salt and freshly ground pepper

40 g (1½ oz) freshly grated
  Parmesan cheese

1 Melt the butter in a large
saucepan, add the pancetta,
onions and garlic and fry for 5
minutes until golden brown. Add
the carrots and celery and cook for
2 minutes.

2 Stir in the haricot beans,
tomatoes and stock. Bring to
boil and simmer, half covered, for
1½–2 hours or until the haricot
beans are tender. If using fresh
peas, add these with the potatoes
after the beans have been cooking
for 1 hour.

3 Add the pasta, French beans,
cabbage, parsley and seasoning. If using frozen peas, add them
at this stage. Simmer for 15
minutes or until the pasta is just
tender. Serve immediately in a
warmed soup tureen, with the
Parmesan cheese handed
separately.

Menu Suggestion
Serve for a winter lunch or supper
meal with fresh bread. A full-
bodied red wine such as Chianti
Classico or Valpolicella goes well
with Minestrone.

MINESTRONE
Correctly speaking, this soup
should be called Minestrone alla
Milanese because it is the classic
soup from Milan—a thick,
wintry vegetable soup with dried
beans and pasta. There are
numerous variations, depending
on the availability of the
vegetables, and sometimes rice is
used instead of pasta. Minestrone
alla Genovese is perhaps the most
famous of these variations, with
its addition of basil and garlic
sauce (pesto) and Pecorino
cheese at the end.

STRACCIATELLA
(CHICKEN BROTH WITH STRANDS OF EGG AND PARMESAN)

0.15	128 cals

Serves 4

1 litre (1¾ pints) chicken stock (see
    page 148) or two 450 ml (15 fl oz)
    cans chicken consommé

3 eggs

45 ml (3 tbsp) freshly grated
    Parmesan cheese

15 ml (1 tbsp) semolina

pinch of freshly grated nutmeg

salt and freshly ground pepper

1 In a large saucepan, heat the
chicken stock or consommé to
barely simmering point.

2 In a separate bowl, beat the
eggs, then add the Parmesan,
semolina, nutmeg and seasoning.
Add a cupful of the hot stock or
consommé and stir until smooth.

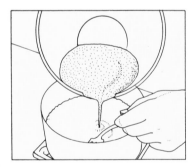

3 Pour the mixture slowly into
the pan of simmering stock,
beating vigorously with a fork for
3–4 minutes.

4 Leave to stand for 2 minutes
to set the egg strands completely. Serve hot, in warmed
individual soup bowls.

Menu Suggestion
Serve as a starter with Scaloppine
al Limone (page 82) to follow for
the main course, and fresh fruit
and cheese to finish.

CIPOLLATA
(ONION SOUP WITH BACON, TOMATOES AND PARMESAN)

| 2.00 | 🍴 | £ | ✳ | 519 cals |

Serves 4

45 ml (3 tbsp) olive oil

100 g (4 oz) unsmoked streaky bacon, rinded and finely diced

800 g (1¾ lb) onions, skinned and finely sliced

1 litre (1¾ pints) chicken stock (see page 148) or two 450 ml (15 fl oz) cans chicken consommé

396 g (14 oz) can tomatoes with their juice

1 small fresh chilli, seeded and finely chopped

salt and freshly ground pepper

30 ml (2 tbsp) roughly chopped basil leaves

45 ml (3 tbsp) freshly grated Parmesan cheese

8 slices French bread, toasted

1 garlic clove, skinned and halved

1 Heat the oil in a large saucepan and fry the bacon for 2–3 minutes, but do not let it brown.

2 Add the onions, stir, then cover the pan and cook on a very low heat for about 1 hour, until the onions are almost melted. Watch the onions carefully and stir them frequently in case they catch and burn.

3 Add the chicken stock, tomatoes, chilli, salt and pepper to taste, cover and cook gently for 30 minutes.

4 Just before serving, stir in the roughly chopped basil leaves and the grated Parmesan cheese.

5 To serve. Rub the toasted bread with the cut sides of the garlic. Put two slices of bread per person in each of four warmed soup bowls.

6 Taste and adjust the seasoning of the soup, then pour over the bread. Serve immediately.

Menu Suggestion

Serve this meal-in-a-bowl soup for lunch or supper with a selection of Italian cheeses to follow and fresh fruit to finish.

CIPOLLATA

Soups are usually eaten with the evening meal in Italy. The main meal of the day is at lunchtime, so in the evening a bowl of soup with some fresh bread is often all that is called for. This soup from the region of Umbria just north of Rome is typical of the kind that Italians enjoy for their evening meal.

There is another version which uses the same ingredients except that it is a thick mixture which is piled onto hot toast and eaten like a savoury. In Umbria, it is eaten as a first course, but it is quite substantial and so must be followed by something light. Make it exactly as the soup on this page, but omit the stock in step 3, then in step 4 combine the Parmesan cheese with 3 beaten eggs and whisk into the mixture off the heat—it should be rather like scrambled eggs.

MINESTRA DI FAGIOLI
(BEAN SOUP)

| 3.00* | £ | ✳ | 152 cals |

* plus overnight soaking

Serves 6

225 g (8 oz) dried white haricot beans, soaked overnight

1.7 litres (3 pints) chicken stock (see page 148) or water

salt and freshly ground pepper

30 ml (2 tbsp) olive oil

2 garlic cloves, skinned and chopped

45 ml (3 tbsp) chopped parsley

extra olive oil, to garnish

1 Drain and rinse the beans, then tip into a large saucepan. Cover with the stock or water and bring to the boil. Simmer, half covered, for 2–2½ hours.

2 Remove half the beans and purée in an electric blender with a little cooking liquid. Return to pan and season.

3 Heat the 30 ml (2 tbsp) olive oil in a small pan, add garlic and fry gently until soft. Stir in parsley, then add to soup.

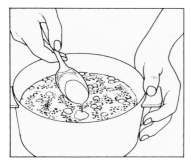

4 Pour the hot soup into a warmed soup tureen, drizzle over a little olive oil and serve.

Menu Suggestion
Serve this substantial soup as a starter before a main course of Abbachio alla Romana (page 88).

PASTA IN BRODO
(PASTA SHAPES IN CHICKEN OR BEEF STOCK)

| 0.20 | £ | 284 cals |

Serves 6

1. 4 litres (2½ pints) chicken or beef
   stock (see page 148) or three
   450 ml (15 fl oz) cans consommé
400 g (14 oz) medium pasta shapes,
   e.g. fusilli, farfalle, conchiglie
salt and freshly ground pepper
freshly grated Parmesan cheese,
   to serve

1 In a large pan, bring the
chicken or beef stock or the
consommé to the boil.

2 Add the pasta and cook for
8–12 minutes (according to
size) until just tender.

3 To serve. Taste and adjust
seasoning, then pour into six
warmed soup bowls. Serve
immediately with freshly grated
Parmesan cheese handed
separately.

Menu Suggestion
Serve this light soup as a starter
with Braciole di Maiale (page 84)
to follow as the main course, and
fresh fruit to finish the meal.

ANTIPASTO MISTO
(ITALIAN MIXED SALAD)

| 0.30* | £ £ | 347 cals* |

* plus 2 hours refrigeration and 20 minutes standing time; 394 cals with optional ingredients

Serves 6

1 head radicchio (see page 136) or a small lettuce

12 thin slices of Italian salami

6 thin slices of Mortadella sausage

6 thin slices of Parma ham

170 g (6 oz) Mozzarella cheese

3 hard-boiled eggs, quartered

3 tomatoes, sliced

160 g (5½ oz) can of mussels in oil (optional)

280 g (10 oz) jar of artichoke hearts in oil (optional)

280 g (10 oz) jar of sweet and sour peppers (optional)

olives and anchovies, to garnish

bread sticks, to serve

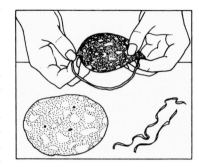

1 Wash the radicchio or lettuce leaves; drain well and pat dry with kitchen paper. Coarsely shred the leaves.

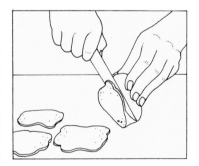

2 Using a sharp knife, carefully cut the Mozzarella cheese into thin slices.

3 Ease any skin or rind off the salami and the Mortadella sausage with your fingers.

4 Place a bed of radicchio or lettuce on a large serving platter. Arrange the slices of salami, Mortadella, Parma ham, Mozzarella, hard-boiled eggs, tomatoes, mussels, artichoke hearts, and peppers on top. Garnish with black olives and anchovies.

5 Cover tightly with cling film and refrigerate for at least 2 hours. Leave at cool room temperature for about 20 minutes before serving.

Menu Suggestion
Serve as a starter for a dinner party meal with Pollo alla Valdostana (page 90) to follow, and Granita All' Arancia (page 124) to finish.

ANTIPASTO MISTO

The word 'antipasto' means 'before the meal', and it can be anything from one or two slices of salami to a huge selection of cold meats, fish, eggs, vegetables and salads. For everyday meals, most Italian families have the simplest of antipasto, say a slice or two of cold meat and hard-boiled eggs with some olives and fresh bread—just enough to whet the appetite before the pasta course.

PROSCIUTTO CON MELONE
(PARMA HAM WITH MELON)

| 0.20 | f f | 104 cals |

Serves 4

900 g (2 lb) Cantaloupe melon
8 thin slices of Parma ham
freshly ground black pepper

1 Cut the melon in half lengthways. Scoop out the seeds from the centre.

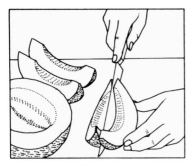

2 Cut each of the melon halves into four even-sized wedge shapes.

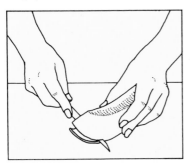

3 With a sharp, pointed knife and using a sawing action, separate the flesh from the skin, keeping it in position on the skin.

4 Cut the flesh across into bite-sized slices, then push each slice in opposite directions.

5 Carefully roll up each of the eight slices of Parma ham. Place two wedges of melon and two rolls of ham on each plate. Grind pepper over the ham before serving.

Menu Suggestion
Serve as a starter for a dinner party meal with Manzo Stufato al Vino Rosso (page 80) for the main course and Granita al Limone (page 124) for the dessert.

——— VARIATION ———

Instead of the melon, use fresh figs in season to make Prosciutto Con Fichi. Only use very fresh, ripe figs in peak condition. In Italy, figs are often served whole and unpeeled, but to help guests who are not used to eating figs as much as the Italians are, it is best to peel them first, then cut them in half. For four people, 8–12 figs is sufficient. Arrange them cut-side up on individual serving plates next to the Parma ham, which may or may not be rolled up, according to how you like it.

BAGNA CAUDA
(HOT ANCHOVY DIP)

| 0.45 | 396 cals |

Serves 6

225 g (8 oz) asparagus, washed, trimmed and freshly cooked

3 globe artichokes, trimmed and freshly cooked

1 small cauliflower

1 large red pepper

1 large green pepper

4 carrots, peeled

6 celery sticks, trimmed

3 courgettes, trimmed

1 bunch radishes

150 ml ($\frac{1}{4}$ pint) olive oil

75 g (3 oz) butter

2 garlic cloves, skinned and finely chopped

two 50 g (2 oz) cans anchovy fillets, drained and finely chopped

1 While the asparagus and artichokes are cooling, prepare the remaining vegetables. Cut the cauliflower into florets, discarding any tough stalks.

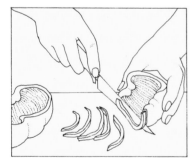

2 Cut the peppers in half lengthways and remove the cores and seeds. Wash the peppers inside and out, dry and cut into strips.

3 Cut the carrots, celery and courgettes into finger-sized sticks. Trim the radishes.

4 Heat the oil and butter in a saucepan until just melted, but not foaming. Add the garlic and cook gently for 2 minutes. Do not allow it to colour.

5 Add the anchovies and cook very gently, stirring all the time, for 10 minutes or until the anchovies dissolve into a paste.

6 To serve. Transfer the dip to an earthenware dish and keep warm over a fondue burner or spirit lamp at the table. Each guest dips the vegetables in the hot anchovy sauce.

Menu Suggestion
Serve as a starter with Triglie al Cartoccio (page 77) to follow as the main course and Budino di Ricotta alla Romana (page 118) for dessert.

FUNGHI RIPIENI AL FORNO
(BAKED STUFFED MUSHROOMS)

| 0.40 | £ £ | 267 cals |

Serves 4

4 rashers of pancetta (see page 133) or unsmoked streaky bacon, rinded

12 large cup mushrooms

75 g (3 oz) fresh white breadcrumbs

1 egg, beaten

30 ml (2 tbsp) chopped fresh parsley

150 ml ($\frac{1}{4}$ pint) dry white wine

salt and freshly ground pepper

90 ml (6 tbsp) freshly grated Parmesan cheese

15 g ($\frac{1}{2}$ oz) butter

1 Make the stuffing mixture. Fry the pancetta in a heavy-based pan until the fat runs, then continue frying until beginning to brown. Remove from the pan and leave to cool for 5 minutes.

2 Meanwhile, carefully remove the stalks from each of the mushrooms, leaving the cups intact.

3 Chop the stalks finely, then put them in a bowl with the breadcrumbs, egg, parsley and 15 ml (1 tbsp) of the wine.

4 With kitchen scissors, snip the cooled pancetta finely into the breadcrumb mixture. Mix well, adding seasoning to taste. Take care not to add too much salt if using pancetta, as this can be quite salty.

5 Place the mushrooms in a single layer in a buttered oven-proof dish and top with the stuffing mixture. Sprinkle with the Parmesan and dot with the butter.

6 Pour the remaining wine into the dish and bake in the oven at 190°C (375°F) mark 5 for 15–20 minutes. Serve hot.

Menu Suggestion
Serve as a starter followed by Scaloppine al Limone (page 82), then Cassata (page 126).

FUNGHI RIPIENI AL FORNO

It is important to buy the right kind of mushrooms for this dish. Button mushrooms are far too small to stuff and they have very little flavour for a dish such as this one. The cup mushrooms specified in this recipe are culti-vated in much the same way as button mushrooms, but they are larger and slightly stronger in flavour. Do not confuse them with the large open mushrooms which would be too strong in flavour and too flat to hold the stuffing.

UOVE TONNATE
(HARD-BOILED EGGS STUFFED WITH TUNA FISH MAYONNAISE)

| 0.25 | 🍳 | £ | 473 cals |

Serves 4

1 egg yolk

salt and freshly ground pepper

100 ml (4 fl oz) olive oil

juice of ½ a lemon

50 g (2 oz) canned tuna fish in oil, drained

6 hard-boiled eggs, shelled

shredded radicchio (see page 136) or curly endive, to serve

black olives, stoned, to garnish

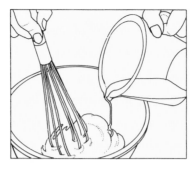

3 Add the rest of the oil in a thin, steady stream, beating, until mayonnaise is thick. Set aside.

4 Halve the hard-boiled eggs lengthways and scoop out the yolks with a teaspoon.

1 Make the mayonnaise. Beat the egg yolk in a bowl with a pinch of salt. Add the olive oil drop by drop, beating well between each addition. Do not add the oil too fast or the mayonnaise will curdle.

2 Once half the oil has been added and the egg yolk is beginning to thicken, add 10 ml (2 tsp) lemon juice and beat well. The mayonnaise should turn pale and become slightly thinner.

5 Sieve or mash the tuna fish and add it to the mayonnaise with the hard-boiled egg yolks, mixing well. Add seasoning to taste, with more lemon juice if necessary.

6 To serve. Fill the cavities of the hard-boiled eggs by piping or spooning in the mayonnaise mixture. Arrange radicchio or endive on individual plates, then place the filled eggs on top. Garnish each egg with slivers of black olive.

Menu Suggestion
Serve before a main course of Bistecche alla Pizzaiola (page 79) and Pesche Ripiene (page 113).

UOVE TONNATE

These stuffed eggs are substantial enough to be served on their own, but they would also make an attractive addition to an antipasto misto. Tuna fish is a popular starter in Italy, but you can vary this according to your own personal taste. Mashed prawns, shrimps or mussels could be substituted for the tuna—the inexpensive kind pickled in brine, which are sold in cans or jars in Italian delicatessens, are perfectly adequate for this dish, combined with a well-flavoured mayonnaise.

INSALATA DI FRUTTI DI MARE
(SEAFOOD SALAD)

| 1.05* | 🥄 | £ £ | 443 cals |

* plus 2 hours chilling

Serves 6

1.1 litres (2 pints) fresh mussels, cleaned and cooked, with cooking liquor reserved (see page 142)

2.8 litres (5 pints) water

1 onion, skinned and roughly chopped

1 bay leaf

salt and freshly ground pepper

350 g (12 oz) squid, cleaned (see page 141)

350 g (12 oz) shelled scallops

350 g (12 oz) peeled prawns, thawed and thoroughly dried if frozen

1 small green pepper, cored, seeded and finely sliced into strips

1 small red pepper, cored, seeded and finely sliced into strips

1 carrot, peeled

150 ml ($\frac{1}{4}$ pint) olive oil

60 ml (4 tbsp) lemon juice

30 ml (2 tbsp) capers

45 ml (3 tbsp) chopped fresh parsley

1 garlic clove, skinned and crushed

black olives, to garnish

1 In a large saucepan, mix together the cooking liquor from the mussels and 1.75 litres (3 pints) of the measured water. Add the onion, bay leaf and a pinch of salt and bring to the boil. Add the squid and simmer gently for 20 minutes or until tender.

2 Remove the squid from the cooking liquid in the pan and set aside.

3 Bring the liquid back to the boil, add the scallops and poach gently for 3 minutes. Remove the scallops from the liquid with a slotted spoon and set aside. (Reserve the fish liquid for making a fish soup.)

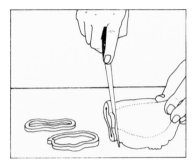

4 Using a sharp knife, cut the squid into rings approximately 1 cm ($\frac{1}{2}$ inch) wide.

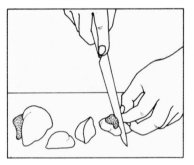

5 Cut the scallops into four, removing the tough muscle (found near the coral or roe).

6 Reserve a few mussels in their shells for the garnish. Remove the shells from the remaining mussels and put the mussels in a large serving bowl with the squid, prawns and scallops. Add the sliced peppers.

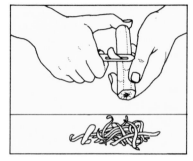

7 With a potato peeler, shred the carrot into ribbons and add this to the seafood.

8 Make the dressing. Mix together the oil, lemon juice, capers, parsley and garlic—with pepper to taste. Pour over the seafood. Mix lightly but thoroughly. Taste and add salt if necessary.

9 To serve. Chill for at least 2 hours and then serve garnished with black olives and the reserved mussels in shells.

Menu Suggestion
Serve for a dinner party starter with Pollo al Rosmarino (page 91) for the main course and Zuccotto (page 114) for dessert.

INSALATA DI FRUTTI DI MARE

All the fish and shellfish specified in this recipe are available at most high-class fishmongers, but if you have difficulty finding one particular kind it isn't absolutely necessary to follow the recipe to the letter. Italian seafood salads vary enormously, depending on the time of year and the availability of fresh fish and shellfish—Italian cooks would far rather make a salad from one top-quality fish than a mixture of inferior ones. Freshness and quality are the keynotes with any Italian seafood dish, and this is worth bearing in mind when shopping—mussels, squid and scallops all have their own 'seasons', so it is worth checking with your fishmonger before buying.

PERE AL GORGONZOLA
(GORGONZOLA STUFFED PEARS)

0.30	607 cals

Serves 4

100 g (4 oz) Gorgonzola cheese, at room temperature

25 g (1 oz) unsalted butter, softened

50 g (2 oz) shelled walnuts, finely chopped

salt and freshly ground pepper

150 ml ($\frac{1}{4}$ pint) thick homemade mayonnaise (see page 147)

about 15 ml (1 tbsp) tarragon vinegar

2 ripe firm pears (e.g. Packham)

juice of $\frac{1}{2}$ a lemon

lettuce leaves, to serve

1 Make the stuffing mixture. Work half the cheese and the butter together with a fork. Add half of the walnuts and pepper to taste and mix together until well combined. (Do not add salt as the cheese is quite salty enough.)

2 Soften the remaining cheese and work it into the mayonnaise. Stir the tarragon vinegar into the mayonnaise mixture to thin it down to a light coating consistency. If too thick, add a little more vinegar. Taste and adjust seasoning.

3 Peel the two pears and, using a sharp knife, cut each one in half lengthways.

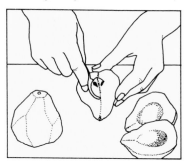

4 Scoop out the cores and a little of the surrounding flesh with a sharp-edged teaspoon. Immediately brush lemon juice over the exposed flesh to prevent discoloration.

5 Fill the scooped-out centres of the pears with the Gorgonzola stuffing mixture.

6 To serve, place 1–2 lettuce leaves in the centre of each individual serving plate. Place one pear half, cut side down, on the lettuce. Coat the pears with the mayonnaise, then sprinkle with the remaining chopped walnuts. Serve immediately.

Menu Suggestion
Serve as a dinner party starter followed by Osso Buco (page 83) and Granita di Caffè (page 124).

TONNO E FAGIOLI
(TUNA FISH WITH BEANS)

2.30* £ 316 cals

* plus overnight soaking

Serves 4

175 g (6 oz) dried white haricot or
  cannellini beans, soaked in cold
  water overnight

45 ml (3 tbsp) olive oil

15 ml (1 tbsp) wine vinegar

salt and freshly ground pepper

1 small onion, skinned and finely
  sliced

200 g (7 oz) can tuna fish in oil,
  drained and flaked into large
  chunks

chopped fresh parsley, to garnish

1 Drain the beans, rinse under
cold running water, then tip
into a large saucepan and cover
with fresh cold water. Bring to the
boil, then lower the heat and
simmer gently for 1½–2 hours or
until beans are tender. Drain.

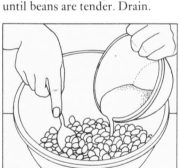

2 Whisk together the oil,
vinegar, salt and pepper and
mix with the hot beans. Cool for
15 minutes.

3 Mix in the onion, then the
tuna fish, being careful not to
break it up too much.

4 To serve. Taste and adjust
seasoning, then transfer to a
serving dish. Sprinkle liberally
with chopped fresh parsley just
before serving.

Menu Suggestion
Serve before a main course of
Pollo al Finocchio (page 95) and a
dessert of Torta di Mele (page
123).

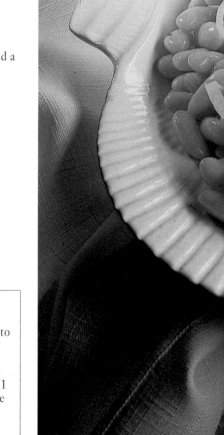

TONNO E FAGIOLI

Both dried white haricot beans
and cannellini are used extensively in Italian cooking—mostly
in salads and soups. Soaking is
essential with dried beans, but if
you forget to soak them overnight, there is an emergency
soaking procedure which works
just as well. Put the beans in a
large saucepan of cold water

(never add salt before cooking
beans as this causes their skins to
toughen) and bring to the boil.
Boil steadily for at least 10
minutes, then remove from the
heat, cover and leave for about 1
hour or until the water has gone
cold. Proceed with the recipe
from step 1.

Pasta, Rice and Gnocchi

In Italy, pasta, rice and gnocchi are eaten as a first course (*primo piatto*). This may seem rather substantial to those of us who are unused to it, but it must be remembered that Italian meals are invariably leisurely affairs, and portions are always kept quite small, so appetites are still keen for the main course. Most of the recipes in this chapter give quantities sufficient for serving pasta and rice dishes as a main course. To serve as a first course, decrease the quantity of pasta or rice to 50–75 g (2–3 oz) per person.

SPAGHETTI ALLA CARBONARA
(SPAGHETTI WITH EGGS AND BACON)

| 0.20 | 683 cals |

Serves 4

30 ml (2 tbsp) olive oil

1 onion, skinned and finely chopped

1 garlic clove, skinned and crushed

400 g (14 oz) spaghetti or other long thin pasta (see pages 130–131)

6 rashers pancetta (see page 133) or unsmoked streaky bacon, rinded and cut into thin strips

60 ml (4 tbsp) dry white wine (optional)

3 eggs

60 ml (4 tbsp) freshly grated Parmesan cheese

30 ml (2 tbsp) single cream

30 ml (2 tbsp) chopped fresh parsley

salt and freshly ground pepper

1 Heat the oil in a pan, add the onion and fry gently for 5 minutes until soft but not coloured. Add the garlic and cook for a further minute.

2 Cook the spaghetti in a large pan of boiling salted water for 8–10 minutes or until just tender.

3 Meanwhile, add the bacon to the onion and fry for 2 minutes over high heat. Add the wine, if using, and boil until evaporated.

4 In a bowl, lightly beat the eggs with the Parmesan, cream, chopped parsley and salt and pepper to taste.

5 Drain the spaghetti, return to the pan with the bacon and onion mixture. Mix well over moderate heat for 1 minute.

6 Remove from the heat and pour in egg mixture, mixing well. The heat from the spaghetti will cook the egg. Turn into a warmed serving dish and serve immediately.

Menu Suggestion
Serve for a family supper with fresh French bread and a green or mixed salad (see box below).

SPAGHETTI ALLA CARBONARA

This recipe originated in the region of Lazio—it is very popular in the capital city of Rome. The Romans happily eat Spaghetti alla Carbonara as a first course before their main meal of meat or fish and vegetables, but if you find this a little heavy going you can serve this quantity for a lunch or supper dish followed by a mixed or green salad and fresh bread. It's the perfect last-minute dish if you have eggs and bacon in the house, because it can be prepared in less than half an hour with hardly any effort and very few other ingredients. Remember it next time everyone's hungry, and serve it as an unusual alternative to fried eggs and bacon.

31

LASAGNE AL FORNO
(PASTA LAYERED WITH MINCED BEEF AND BÉCHAMEL SAUCE)

| 2.10 | £ | ✳* | 571–856 cals |

* freeze after step 5

Serves 4–6

30 ml (2 tbsp) olive oil

1 onion, skinned and finely chopped

50 g (2 oz) carrot, peeled and finely chopped

100 g (4 oz) button mushrooms, wiped and sliced

50 g (2 oz) pancetta (see page 133) or unsmoked streaky bacon, rinded and finely diced

1 garlic clove, skinned and crushed

450 g (1 lb) lean minced beef or veal

350 g (12 oz) fresh tomatoes, skinned, seeded and sieved, or 226 g (8 oz) can tomatoes

15 ml (1 tbsp) tomato purée

150 ml ($\frac{1}{4}$ pint) dry white wine

150 ml ($\frac{1}{4}$ pint) beef stock

2 bay leaves

salt and freshly ground pepper

900 ml (1$\frac{1}{2}$ pints) milk

slices of onion, carrot and celery

6 peppercorns

100 g (4 oz) butter

75 g (3 oz) plain flour

12–15 sheets oven-ready lasagne (see box)

50 g (2 oz) freshly grated Parmesan cheese

1 Heat the oil in a large, heavy saucepan, add the onion, carrot, mushrooms, pancetta and crushed garlic. Fry, stirring, for 1–2 minutes. Add the beef or veal and cook over high heat for a further 2 minutes.

2 Stir in the tomatoes and juices, tomato purée, wine, beef stock, 1 bay leaf and seasoning to taste. Bring to the boil, reduce the heat to a simmer, cover and cook for about 35 minutes.

3 Meanwhile, pour the milk into a saucepan, add a few slices of onion, carrot and celery, the peppercorns and remaining bay leaf. Bring slowly to the boil, then remove from heat, cover and leave to infuse for about 15 minutes.

4 Make the béchamel sauce. Strain the infused milk into a jug. Melt the butter in a saucepan, add the flour and cook over low heat, stirring with a wooden spoon, for 2 minutes. Remove the pan from the heat and gradually blend in the milk, stirring after each addition to prevent lumps forming. Bring to the boil slowly and continue to cook for 2–3 minutes, stirring all the time until the sauce thickens. Add seasoning to taste.

5 Brush the inside of a baking dish with butter. Spoon one third of the meat sauce over the base of the dish. Cover this with 4–5 sheets of lasagne and spread over one third of the béchamel. Repeat these layers twice more, finishing with the béchamel sauce which should cover the lasagne completely. Sprinkle grated Parmesan over the top.

6 Stand the dish on a baking sheet. Bake in the oven at 180°C (350°F) mark 4 for about 45 minutes or until the top is well browned and bubbling.

Menu Suggestion
Serve as a main course dish followed by tomato and green salads, and a light dessert such as fresh fruit or Granita All' Arancia (page 124).

LASAGNE AL FORNO

There are numerous different recipes for lasagne al forno (lasagne baked in the oven): many like this one which combine layers of meat sauce, béchamel and pasta; some with three different cheeses (Parmesan, Mozzarella and Bel Paese) instead of the béchamel, and others with meatballs instead of meat sauce.

This recipe uses oven-ready lasagne, which is easy to use and saves preparation time. It is widely available both at super-markets and delicatessens and needs no pre-cooking — you simply take it straight from the box and layer it with the béchamel and meat sauces. The same thing can be done with homemade lasagne, which gives a beautiful light result and is well worth making for a dish such as this one which is heavy with other ingredients.

If only the ordinary dried lasagne is available this can of course be used, but you will find it time-consuming and messy, because it has to be boiled in batches before it can be layered with the other ingredients. Always boil it in a very large pan, in *plenty* of boiling salted water (to prevent sticking). Adding 15 ml (1 tbsp) vegetable oil to the water before putting in the lasagne also helps with this problem. Only cook a few sheets at a time (4–6 at the most) to avoid overcrowding the pan, then drain and dry the sheets on a clean tea towel before layering them.

RAVIOLI
(PASTA FILLED WITH RICOTTA AND SPINACH)

$\boxed{1.30}$ $\boxed{\,}$ $\boxed{\text{\large *}}$* $\boxed{733 \text{ cals}}$

* freeze after step 7

Serves 4

350 g (12 oz) washed fresh spinach
 or 175 g (6 oz) frozen spinach

175 g (6 oz) Ricotta or curd cheese

115 g (4½ oz) freshly grated
 Parmesan

1 egg, beaten

pinch of freshly grated nutmeg or
 ground allspice

salt and freshly ground pepper

basic pasta dough made with 3
 eggs and 300 g (11 oz) plain flour
 (see page 150)

75 g (3 oz) butter

a few fresh sage leaves, chopped,
 and a few extra, to garnish

1 Make the pasta stuffing. Place
the spinach in a saucepan
without any water and cook gently
for 5–10 minutes, or until thawed
if using frozen spinach. Drain very
well and chop the spinach finely.

2 Mix together the spinach,
Ricotta or curd cheese, 65 g
(2½ oz) Parmesan, the egg, nutmeg
and seasoning.

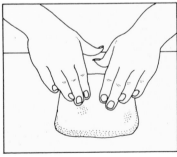

3 Cut the dough in two. Wrap
one half in cling film. Pat the
other half out to a rectangle, then
roll out firmly to an even sheet of
almost paper-thin pasta. If pasta
sticks, ease it carefully and flour
lightly underneath. Make sure
there are no holes or creases.
Cover with a clean damp cloth and
repeat with other half of dough.

4 Working quickly to prevent
the pasta drying out, place tea-
spoonfuls of the filling evenly
spaced at 4 cm (1½ inch) intervals
across and down the sheet of
dough that has just been rolled
out and is not covered.

5 With a pastry brush or your
index finger, glaze the spaces
between the filling with beaten
egg or water—this is of great
importance as it acts as a bond to
seal the ravioli.

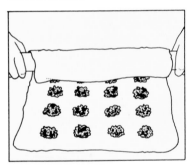

6 Uncover the other sheet of
pasta, carefully lift this on the
rolling-pin (to avoid stretching)
and unroll it over the first sheet,
easing gently. Press down firmly
around the pockets of filling and
along the dampened lines to push
out any trapped air and seal well.

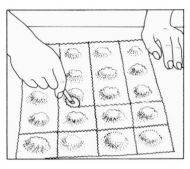

7 With a ravioli cutter, serrated-
edged wheel or even a sharp
knife, cut the ravioli into squares
between the pouches. Lift the
ravioli one by one on to a well-
floured baking sheet and leave to
dry for about 1 hour before cooking (or cover with cling film and
refrigerate overnight).

8 Pour at least 2.3 litres (4 pints)
water into a large saucepan
and bring to the boil. Add 10 ml
(2 tsp) salt.

9 Add the ravioli a few at a time,
stirring so that they do not
stick together. (A few drops of oil
added to the water will stop it
boiling over.) Cook the ravioli at a
gentle boil for about 5 minutes
until just tender. Remove with a
slotted spoon and place in a
warmed buttered serving dish.
Keep hot while cooking the remainder of the ravioli.

10 Melt the measured butter
in a saucepan and stir in the
rest of the grated Parmesan cheese
with the chopped sage. Pour over
the ravioli and toss to coat evenly.
Serve immediately, garnished with
fresh sage.

Menu Suggestion
Serve as a first course before
Sogliole al Marsala (page 78) and
Pesche Ripiene (page 113).

CANNELLONI
(PASTA FILLED WITH BEEF AND CHEESE)

0.45	🗎	✳*	998–1444 cals

* freeze after step 7

Serves 4–6

15 g ($\frac{1}{2}$ oz) butter

30 ml (2 tbsp) vegetable oil

1 onion, skinned and chopped

50 g (2 oz) pancetta (see page 133)
   or unsmoked streaky bacon,
   rinded and chopped

350 g (12 oz) lean minced beef

15 ml (1 tbsp) tomato purée

150 ml ($\frac{1}{4}$ pint) red wine

2 egg yolks

pinch of freshly grated nutmeg

225 g (8 oz) Ricotta or curd cheese

50 g (2 oz) freshly grated
   Parmesan cheese

salt and freshly ground pepper

1.1 litres (2 pints) béchamel sauce
   (see page 148)

12–18 tubes oven-ready cannelloni

parsley sprigs, to garnish

1 Melt the butter and oil in a medium, heavy saucepan, add onion and fry for 5 minutes until soft but not coloured. Add pancetta and cook for 2 minutes.

2 Add the beef, increase the heat and cook until well browned, removing any lumps with a fork.

3 Stir in tomato purée and red wine. Cook, stirring, until most of liquid has evaporated. Set aside to cool for 10 minutes.

4 Mix together the meat, egg yolks, nutmeg, Ricotta, 25 g (1 oz) Parmesan and seasoning.

5 Pour half of the béchamel sauce into a shallow oven-proof dish which will take the cannelloni in a single layer.

6 With a spoon, fill the cannelloni with the meat. Lay them side by side in the dish. Coat with remaining béchamel, sprinkle over remaining cheese and bake at 200°C (400°F) mark 6 for 20 minutes.

Menu Suggestion
Serve as a first course before Triglie al Cartoccio (page 77). Finish the meal with fresh fruit.

FETTUCCINE ALLE VONGOLE
(FETTUCCINE WITH CLAM SAUCE)

| 0.45 | f f | 565 cals |

Serves 4

15 ml (1 tbsp) olive oil

1 onion, skinned and finely chopped

2–3 garlic cloves, skinned and crushed

700 g (1½ lb) tomatoes, skinned and roughly chopped, or one 397 g (14 oz) can tomatoes

two 200 g (7 oz) cans or jars baby clams in brine, drained (see box)

30 ml (2 tbsp) chopped fresh parsley

salt and freshly ground pepper

400 g (14 oz) fettuccine or other long thin pasta (see pages 130–131)

1 Make the sauce. Heat 15 ml (1 tbsp) olive oil in a saucepan, add the onion and garlic and fry gently for 5 minutes until soft but not coloured.

2 Stir in the tomatoes and their juice, bring to the boil and cook for 15–20 minutes until slightly reduced.

3 Stir the drained clams into the sauce with 15 ml (1 tbsp) parsley and salt and pepper to taste. Remove from the heat.

4 Cook the fettuccine in a large pan of boiling salted water for 8–10 minutes until just tender.

5 Reheat the sauce just before the pasta is cooked, and taste and adjust seasoning. Drain the fettuccine well, tip into a warmed serving dish and pour over the clam sauce. Sprinkle with the remaining chopped parsley to garnish.

Menu Suggestion
Serve as a lunch or supper dish with fresh bread rolls and a bottle of chilled dry white wine such as Frascati. Follow with Insalata di Finocchi e Cetrioli (page 109).

FETTUCCINE ALLE VONGOLE

Fresh clams are easy to obtain in Italy, and are preferred for making this delicious sauce. If you are able to get fresh clams, so much the better. For this sauce, you will need about 2.3 litres (4 pints). Scrub them under cold running water with a stiff brush and scrape off any barnacles with a knife. Discard any clams which are not tightly closed, then put the remainder in a colander and leave them under running water for 20 minutes. Put the clams in a large saucepan with 300 ml (½ pint) water, cover and bring to the boil. Cook over high heat until all the shells are open (about 10 minutes), shaking the pan occasionally. If some remain closed after this time, discard them. Strain the clams, discarding the cooking liquid. Remove the meat from the shells (reserving a few whole ones to garnish, if liked), then use in step 3 of the recipe as drained canned clams.

TORTELLINI ALLA PANNA
(TORTELLINI WITH CREAM)

2.15 ⊟ £ £ ✳ 730 cals

Serves 6

50 g (2 oz) butter

275 g (10 oz) chicken breast, skinned, boned and chopped

100 g (4 oz) Parma ham or boiled ham, finely chopped

75 g (3 oz) freshly grated Parmesan cheese

2 eggs, lightly beaten

pinch of freshly grated nutmeg

salt and freshly ground pepper

basic pasta dough made with 3 eggs and 300 g (11 oz) plain flour (see page 150)

30 ml (2 tbsp) vegetable oil

300 ml (10 fl oz) double cream

1 Make the chicken filling. Melt 25 g (1 oz) butter in a large frying pan and cook the chicken for about 5 minutes or until tender. Remove from the heat and leave to cool slightly for 10 minutes.

2 Put the chicken in a blender or food processor with the ham, 50 g (2 oz) of the cheese, the eggs, nutmeg and salt and pepper to taste. Work until very finely minced.

3 Cut the prepared dough into two pieces. Wrap each piece in cling film and leave to rest for 20 minutes. Roll out one piece on a well-floured surface to a 66 × 23 cm (29 × 9 inch) rectangle.

4 Cut out rounds with a 5-cm (2-inch) pastry cutter, reserving the trimmings to make more tortellini.

5 Working quickly to prevent the pasta drying out, place 2.5 ml ($\frac{1}{2}$ tsp) of the chicken filling on each round. Brush the edges with water and fold in half, the top edge and the bottom edge not quite meeting. Press together well to seal.

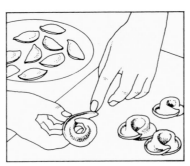

6 Curl the two ends of the semi-circle into a ring around the index finger until the ends touch. At the same time turn the sealed edge of the dough towards the fold to make a groove around the edge. Seal the ends together firmly.

7 Spread the tortellini out in a single layer on a floured tea towel while making the remainder. Leave to dry for 30 minutes before cooking.

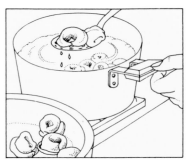

8 Pour at least 2.3 litres (4 pints) water into a large saucepan and bring to the boil. Add the oil and 10 ml (2 tsp) salt, then add the tortellini a few at a time, stirring so that they do not stick together. Cook the tortellini at a gentle boil for about 5 minutes until just tender. Remove with a slotted spoon and place in a warmed buttered serving dish. Keep hot while cooking the remainder of the tortellini.

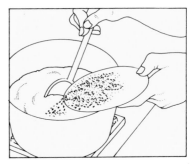

9 In a separate saucepan, melt the rest of the butter, add the cream, bring to the boil and cook until slightly thickened. Stir in the rest of the Parmesan, mix well and then pour over the tortellini. Serve immediately.

Menu Suggestion
Serve as a first course before Manzo Stufato al Vino Rosso (page 80). Finish with Granita al Limone (page 124) for dessert.

TAGLIATELLE CON SALSA AL GORGONZOLA
(TAGLIATELLE WITH GORGONZOLA SAUCE)

0.25	683 cals

Serves 4

25 g (1 oz) butter

175 g (6 oz) Gorgonzola cheese

150 ml ($\frac{1}{4}$ pint) whipping cream

30 ml (2 tbsp) dry white wine

15 ml (1 tbsp) chopped fresh sage

salt and freshly ground pepper

350 g (12 oz) dried tagliatelle or other long thin pasta (pages 130–131)

1 Make the sauce. Melt the butter in a heavy-based saucepan.

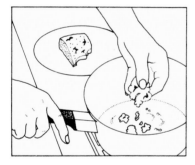

2 Crumble in the Gorgonzola cheese, then stir over gentle heat for 2–3 minutes until melted.

3 Pour in the cream and wine, whisking vigorously. Stir in sage, season and cook, stirring, until sauce thickens. Remove the pan from the heat.

4 Cook the tagliatelle in a large pan of boiling salted water for 8–10 minutes until just tender. Drain thoroughly.

5 Gently reheat the Gorgonzola sauce, whisking vigorously all the time. Taste and adjust seasoning.

6 Divide the tagliatelle equally between four warmed serving bowls. Top each portion with sauce and serve immediately.

Menu Suggestion
Serve as a first course before Pollo alla Diavola (page 92) accompanied by Zucchini in Agrodolce (page 106).

CONCHIGLIE AL MASCARPONE E NOCI
(PASTA SHELLS WITH CHEESE AND WALNUTS)

0.30	644 cals

Serves 4

275 g (10 oz) conchiglie or other
   pasta shapes (see page 131)

salt and freshly ground pepper

25 g (1 oz) butter

225 g (8 oz) Mascarpone (see page
   134) or other full fat soft cheese

30 ml (2 tbsp) freshly grated
   Parmesan cheese

75 g (3 oz) walnuts, roughly
   chopped

1 Cook the conchiglie in a large
pan of boiling salted water for
20 minutes or until just tender.
Drain well.

2 In the same pan, melt the
butter, add the cheese and stir
for about 2–3 minutes until heated
through. Do not boil.

3 Add the Parmesan and
walnuts, stir, then add the
pasta. Mix well until evenly coated
with sauce. Season to taste. Serve
immediately.

Menu Suggestion
Serve as a first course before
Bistecche alla Pizzaiola (page 79)
and fresh fruit for dessert.

PASTICCIO DI MACCHERONI
(*MACARONI PIE*)

1.10	£	587 cals

Serves 6

115 g (4½ oz) butter

30 ml (2 tbsp) olive oil

1 small onion, skinned and finely chopped

2 garlic cloves, skinned and crushed

397 g (14 oz) can tomatoes

5 ml (1 tsp) chopped fresh basil or 2.5 ml (½ tsp) dried, or mixed herbs

salt and freshly ground pepper

225 g (8 oz) large macaroni

75 g (3 oz) plain flour

568 ml (1 pint) milk

75 g (3 oz) Gruyère cheese, grated

1.25 ml (¼ tsp) freshly grated nutmeg

60 ml (4 tbsp) freshly grated Parmesan cheese

45 ml (3 tbsp) dried breadcrumbs

1 Make the tomato sauce. Melt 50 g (2 oz) of the butter in a heavy-based saucepan with the olive oil. Add the onion and garlic and fry gently for 5 minutes until soft but not coloured.

2 Add the tomatoes and their juices with the basil and seasoning to taste, then stir with a wooden spoon to break up the tomatoes. Bring to the boil, then lower the heat and simmer for 10 minutes, stirring occasionally.

3 Meanwhile, plunge the macaroni into a large pan of boiling salted water, bring back to the boil and cook for 10 minutes until just tender.

4 Make the cheese sauce. Melt the remaining butter in a separate saucepan, add the flour and cook over low heat, stirring with a wooden spoon, for about 2 minutes. Remove the pan from the heat and gradually blend in the milk, stirring after each addition to prevent lumps forming. Bring to the boil slowly, stirring all the time until the sauce thickens. Add the Gruyère cheese and seasoning to taste and stir until melted.

5 Drain the macaroni and mix with the tomato sauce. Arrange half of this mixture in a large buttered ovenproof dish.

6 Pour over half of the cheese sauce. Repeat the layers, then sprinkle evenly with the Parmesan and breadcrumbs.

7 Bake the pie in the oven at 190°C (375°F) mark 5 for 15 minutes, then brown under a preheated hot grill for 5 minutes. Serve hot.

Menu Suggestion
Serve for a family supper accompanied by Insalata di Finocchi e Cetrioli (page 109).

RISI E BISI
(RICE AND PEAS)

| 0.30 | 🝳 | 573 cals |

Serves 4

50 g (2 oz) butter

1 small onion, skinned and finely chopped

1.4–1.7 litres (2½–3 pints) chicken stock (see page 148)

50 g (2 oz) pancetta (see page 133) or unsmoked streaky bacon, rinded and chopped

700 g (1½ lb) peas in the pod, shelled, or 350 g (12 oz) frozen petits pois

150 ml (¼ pint) white wine

salt and freshly ground pepper

350 g (12 oz) arborio rice (see page 132)

25 g (1 oz) freshly grated Parmesan cheese

1 Melt 25 g (1 oz) butter in a large, heavy-based saucepan, add the onion and fry gently for 5 minutes until soft but not coloured.

2 Bring the stock to the boil in a separate large saucepan and keep at barely simmering point.

3 Stir the pancetta into the onion, cook for 1 minute, then add the fresh peas, if using, and the wine and seasoning to taste. Cook for 10 minutes, adding a little stock if necessary.

4 Add the rice and the rest of the stock and stir well. Cover and cook for 15–20 minutes until the rice is tender. Stir the rice once or twice during cooking. If using frozen peas, add them 5 minutes before the end of the cooking time.

5 When the rice and peas are tender, stir in the remaining butter and the freshly grated Parmesan cheese. Taste and adjust seasoning.

Menu Suggestion
Serve as a first course before Scaloppine al Limone (page 82) and Zabaglione (page 128).

RISI E BISI

This classic dish is a cross between a risotto and a soup, and is always eaten as a first course in Italy—usually with a fork rather than a soup spoon. It is a speciality of the city of Venice, where it can be seen on almost every restaurant menu. The Venetians are said to be very particular about the way they make their Risi e Bisi, pre-ferring to use only fresh peas in season, and *never* frozen peas. There is no need for us to be so fussy, however, so long as the proportion of peas to rice is correct, and the consistency is half soup, half risotto. You will find it quite delicious as a first course, or even as a lunch or supper dish on its own.

GNOCCHI DI PATATE
(POTATO DUMPLINGS)

| 0.45 | £ | ✳* | 586 cals |

* freeze after step 6

Serves 4

900 g (2 lb) old potatoes

salt

50 g (2 oz) butter

1 egg, beaten

225–275 g (8–10 oz) plain flour

1 quantity Pesto (see page 146) or Salsa di Pomodoro (see page 144), to serve

freshly grated Parmesan cheese, to finish

1 Cook the potatoes in their skins in boiling salted water for about 20 minutes until tender. Drain well.

2 Sieve the potatoes while still warm into a large bowl. Add 5 ml (1 tsp) salt, the butter, egg and half the flour. Mix well to bind the potatoes together.

3 Turn out on to a floured surface, gradually adding more flour and kneading until the dough is soft, smooth and slightly sticky.

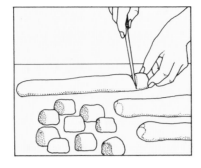

4 With floured hands, roll the dough into 2.5-cm (1-inch) thick ropes. Cut the ropes into 1.5-cm (¾-inch) pieces.

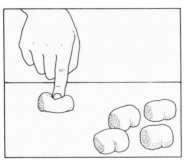

5 Press a finger into each piece to flatten; draw finger towards you to curl sides.

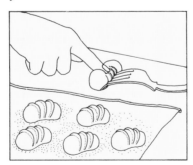

6 Alternatively, you can make a decorative shape by using the same rolling technique, but roll the dumpling over the end of the prongs of a fork. Spread out on a floured tea towel.

7 Bring a large pan of salted water to the boil and reduce to barely simmering. Drop in about twenty-four gnocchi at a time and cook gently for 2–3 minutes or until they float to the surface.

8 With a slotted spoon, remove the gnocchi from the pan, then place them in a buttered serving dish. Cover and keep warm while cooking the remaining gnocchi.

9 When all the gnocchi are cooked, toss them in the chosen sauce. Serve immediately, sprinkled with freshly grated Parmesan.

Menu Suggestion
Serve as a first course for a dinner party with Abbachio alla Romana (page 88) to follow and Cassata (page 126) to finish.

GNOCCHI DI PATATE
Gnocchi are little dumplings, in this recipe made from potatoes although there are other versions made with semolina (gnocchi di semolino), and spinach and ricotta cheese (gnocchi verdi— see page 48). The Italians always eat gnocchi as a first course (primo piatto), sometimes simply sprinkled with melted butter and grated Parmesan cheese, at other times coated in a rich and pungent tomato sauce. The type of gnocchi and the way in which they are served is purely regional; these potato gnocchi are fairly typical of the regions of northern Italy. In Lombardy and Veneto, chopped fresh sage would be added to the melted butter and cheese, whereas in Liguria they like to serve their gnocchi with basil and garlic (pesto) sauce.

GNOCCHI VERDI
(RICOTTA AND SPINACH DUMPLINGS WITH BUTTER AND CHEESE)

0.55	£ ✳*	700 cals

* freeze after step 3

Serves 4

900 g (2 lb) washed fresh spinach
  or 450 g (1 lb) frozen spinach

225 g (8 oz) Ricotta or curd cheese

2 eggs, beaten

225 g (8 oz) plain flour

1.25 ml ($\frac{1}{4}$ tsp) freshly grated
  nutmeg

100 g (4 oz) freshly grated
  Parmesan cheese

salt and freshly ground pepper

100 g (4 oz) butter

1 Place the spinach in a saucepan without any water and cook gently for 5–10 minutes, or until thawed if using frozen spinach. Drain very well and chop the spinach finely.

2 Mix together the Ricotta or curd cheese, eggs, flour, spinach, nutmeg, half the Parmesan and salt and pepper to taste.

3 With floured hands, form the mixture into cork-sized croquettes, or balls the size of large marbles. Chill in the refrigerator for at least 1 hour.

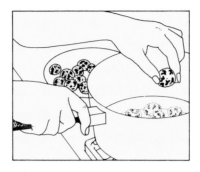

4 Bring a large pan of salted water to the boil and reduce to barely simmering. Drop in 10–12 gnocchi at a time and cook for 8–10 minutes or until they float to the surface.

5 With a slotted spoon, remove the gnocchi from the pan, then place them in a buttered serving dish. Cover and keep warm while cooking the remaining gnocchi.

6 Melt the butter in a small saucepan and pour it over the gnocchi. Sprinkle with the remaining cheese. Serve immediately.

Menu Suggestion
Serve as a first course with Pollo al Finocchio (page 95) for the main course, and Granita di Fragole (page 124) for dessert.

RISOTTO ALLA MILANESE
(SAFFRON RISOTTO)

| 0.35 | 🎩 f | 534 cals |

Serves 4

1.1 litres (2 pints) beef stock (see page 148)

75 g (3 oz) butter

1 small onion, skinned and finely chopped

350 g (12 oz) arborio rice (see page 132)

pinch of saffron strands

salt and freshly ground pepper

50 g (2 oz) freshly grated Parmesan cheese

1 Bring the stock to the boil in a large saucepan and keep at barely simmering point.

2 Meanwhile, in a large, heavy-based saucepan, melt 25 g (1 oz) butter, add the onion and fry gently for 5 minutes until soft but not coloured.

3 Add the arborio rice to the pan and stir well for 2–3 minutes until the rice is well coated with the butter.

4 Add a ladleful of stock to the pan, cook gently, stirring occasionally until the stock is absorbed. Add more stock as soon as each ladleful is absorbed, stirring frequently.

5 When the rice becomes creamy, sprinkle in the saffron with salt and pepper to taste. Continue adding stock and stirring until the risotto is thick and creamy, tender but not sticky. This process should take 20–25 minutes. It must not be hurried.

6 Just before serving, stir in the remaining butter and the Parmesan cheese.

Menu Suggestion
Serve as an accompaniment to Osso Buco (page 83).

Risotto alla Veronese
(MUSHROOM AND HAM RISOTTO)

| 0.50 | 🄳 | £ | 622 cals |

Serves 4

90 g (3½ oz) butter

15 ml (1 tbsp) olive oil

2 small onions, skinned and finely chopped

1 garlic clove, skinned and crushed

225 g (8 oz) mushrooms, wiped and sliced

30 ml (2 tbsp) chopped fresh parsley

150 ml (¼ pint) white wine

900 ml (1½ pints) chicken stock (see page 148)

350 g (12 oz) arborio rice (see page 132)

50 g (2 oz) cooked ham, diced

25 g (1 oz) freshly grated Parmesan cheese

salt and freshly ground pepper

1 Melt 15 g (½ oz) butter and 15 ml (1 tbsp) olive oil in a saucepan. Add half the chopped onion and fry gently for 5 minutes until soft but not coloured.

2 Add the garlic, cook for 1 minute, then add the mushrooms and parsley. Cook gently for 10 minutes until the mushrooms are tender. Stir in 25 g (1 oz) butter and set aside while making the risotto.

3 Bring the stock to the boil in a large saucepan and keep at barely simmering point.

4 In a large, heavy-based saucepan, melt 25 g (1 oz) butter, add the rest of the onion and fry gently for 5 minutes until soft but not coloured.

5 Add the arborio rice and stir well for 2–3 minutes until the rice is well coated with the butter.

6 Add the wine, cook gently, stirring until absorbed. Add 150 ml (¼ pint) of stock as soon as this is absorbed. Continue to add stock in 150 ml (¼ pint) measures, stirring frequently until the risotto is thick and creamy, tender but not sticky. This should take 20–25 minutes. It must not be hurried.

7 Finally, stir in the remaining butter, ham, mushroom mixture and cheese. Taste and adjust seasoning. Serve immediately.

Menu Suggestion

Serve as a first course followed by Sogliole al Marsala (page 78) and Pesche Ripiene (page 113).

51

Pizzas

Pizzas are the perfect convenience food. Cut into wedges, they are easy to eat with the fingers, whereas the plate-sized ones make a substantial meal served with a selection of salads. In Italy they are made in *pizzerie* —special pizza bakeries which have exceptionally hot ovens for making the most perfect of pizza doughs. Most Italians go out to eat pizza, or bring them home for a quick lunch or evening snack. You can do the same too, of course, but it is much more satisfying to make your own pizzas at home —and you can vary the toppings to suit individual tastes.

PIZZA NAPOLETANA
(PIZZA WITH TOMATOES, MOZZARELLA AND ANCHOVIES)

| 1.30* | £ | ✳* | 692 cals |

* plus 1½–2 hours rising; freeze after step 4

Serves 4

1 quantity of basic pizza dough (see page 149)

60 ml (4 tbsp) olive oil

450 g (1 lb) ripe tomatoes, skinned and chopped or 397 g (14 oz) can tomatoes, drained

pinch of sugar, or to taste

salt and freshly ground pepper

225 g (8 oz) Italian Mozzarella cheese, thinly sliced

50 g (2 oz) can anchovy fillets, drained and cut in half lengthways

20 ml (4 tsp) chopped fresh oregano or 10 ml (2 tsp) dried

1 Make the basic pizza dough according to the instructions on page 149 and leave to rise.

2 Put half of the olive oil in a pan with the tomatoes, sugar and salt and pepper to taste. Simmer for about 10 minutes, stirring from time to time.

3 Meanwhile, turn the risen dough out on to a floured surface. Roll out and cut into two 27.5-cm (11-inch) circles. (Use a large plate, flan dish or ring as a guide.) Make the edges slightly thicker than the centres.

4 Put the circles of dough on oiled baking sheets and spread the tomato mixture evenly over them, right to the edges. Arrange the slices of Mozzarella over the tomatoes.

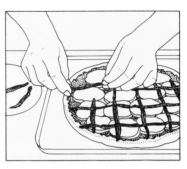

5 Arrange the anchovies in a lattice pattern over the top of the tomatoes.

6 Sprinkle over the remaining oil, with the oregano and salt and pepper to taste. Leave to prove in a warm place for about 30 minutes, then bake in a 220°C (425°F) mark 7 oven for 25 minutes or until the topping is melted and the dough well risen. Swap the baking sheets over halfway through the cooking time. Serve hot or cold.

Menu Suggestion
Serve as a lunch or supper dish with a crisp green salad tossed in an olive oil and lemon juice dressing.

PIZZA QUATTRO STAGIONI
(FOUR SEASONS PIZZA)

| 1.30* | £ | ✳* | 782 cals |

* plus 1½–2 hours rising; freeze after step 6

Makes 4

1 quantity of basic pizza dough (see page 149)

175 g (6 oz) button mushrooms, thinly sliced

45 ml (3 tbsp) olive oil

2 garlic cloves, skinned and crushed

10 ml (2 tsp) chopped fresh basil or 5 ml (1 tsp) dried

450 ml (¾ pint) tomato sauce (see page 144)

16 slices of Italian salami, rinded

50 g (2 oz) black olives, halved and stoned

8 bottled artichoke hearts, sliced

225 g (8 oz) Italian Mozzarella cheese, thinly sliced

4 tomatoes, skinned and sliced

10 ml (2 tsp) chopped fresh oregano or 5 ml (1 tsp) dried

salt and freshly ground pepper

1 Make the basic pizza dough according to the instructions on page 149 and leave to rise.

2 Fry the mushrooms lightly in 30 ml (2 tbsp) of the oil with the garlic and basil.

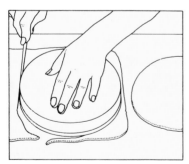

3 Turn the risen dough out on to a floured surface, roll out and cut into four 20-cm (8-inch) circles, using sandwich tins or flan rings as a guide. Make the edges slightly thicker than the centres.

4 Put the circles of dough into oiled sandwich tins. Spread the tomato sauce evenly over dough, right to edges.

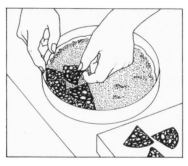

5 Cut each slice of salami into four quarters. Arrange these pieces in one quarter of each pizza, overlapping them to cover tomato sauce. Dot with olives.

6 Arrange the artichokes slices over another pizza quarter, the cheese and tomato over another and mushrooms over the last.

7 Sprinkle the remaining oil over the pizzas with the oregano and seasoning.

8 Leave the pizzas to prove in a warm place for about 30 minutes, then bake in the oven at 220°C (425°F) mark 7 for 25 minutes. Swap over quickly, half-way through the cooking time. Serve hot or cold.

Menu Suggestion
Serve with Insalata di Finocchi e Cetrioli (page 109) for an informal supper.

PIZZA QUATTRO FORMAGGI
(PIZZA WITH FOUR CHEESES)

| 1.30* | £ | ✳* | 803 cals |

* plus 1½–2 hours rising; freeze after
step 5

Makes 4

**1 quantity of basic pizza dough
(see page 149)**

226 g (8 oz) can tomatoes

salt and freshly ground pepper

**100 g (4 oz) Italian Mozzarella
cheese, diced**

**100 g (4 oz) Bel Paese or Provolone
cheese, diced**

100 g (4 oz) Fontina cheese, diced

100 g (4 oz) Taleggio cheese, diced

20 ml (4 tsp) olive oil

**20 ml (4 tsp) chopped fresh mixed
herbs or 10 ml (2 tsp) dried**

1 Make the basic pizza dough
according to the instructions
on page 149 and leave to rise.

2 Turn the risen dough out on
to a floured surface, roll out
and cut into four 20-cm (8-inch)
circles, using sandwich tins or flan
rings as a guide. Make the edges
slightly thicker than the centres.

3 Put dough into oiled sandwich
tins or flan rings placed on
oiled baking sheets.

4 Crush the tomatoes with their
juice and spread evenly over
the dough, right to the edges.
Season to taste.

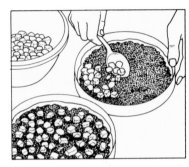

5 Mix the four cheeses together
and sprinkle them evenly over
the four pizzas.

6 Sprinkle over the oil and
herbs, with salt and pepper to
taste. Leave the pizzas to prove in
a warm place for about 30
minutes, then bake in the oven at
220°C (425°F) mark 7 for 25
minutes or until the cheeses are
melted and the dough is well risen.
Swap the oven shelves over half-
way through the cooking time.
Serve hot or cold.

Menu Suggestion
Serve for lunch or supper followed
by cold Peperonata (page 98).

PIZZA CASALINGA
(FARMHOUSE PIZZA)

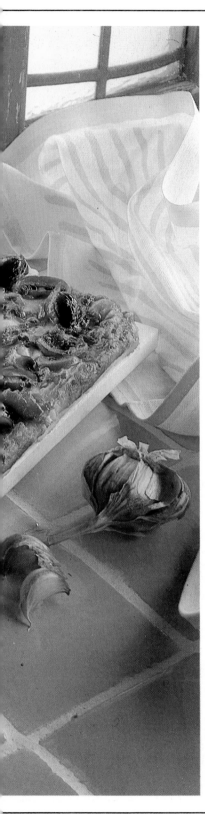

| 1.30 | £ | ✳* | 566 cals |

* plus 1½–2 hours rising; freeze after step 5

Serves 6

1 quantity of basic pizza dough (see page 149)

60 ml (4 tbsp) olive oil

2 garlic cloves, skinned and crushed

225 g (8 oz) mushrooms, wiped

397 g (14 oz) can tomatoes

salt and freshly ground pepper

400 g (14 oz) Italian Mozzarella cheese, thinly sliced

100 g (4 oz) boiled ham, cut into strips

50 g (2 oz) bottled mussels or can anchovy fillets, drained

10 black olives, halved and stoned

20 ml (4 tsp) chopped fresh oregano or 10 ml (2 tsp) dried

1 Make the basic pizza dough according to the instructions on page 149 and leave to rise.

2 Heat 30 ml (2 tbsp) oil in a heavy-based frying pan. Add the garlic and mushrooms and fry for about 5 minutes until the oil is completely absorbed.

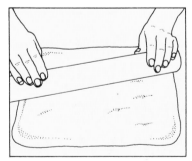

3 Turn the risen dough out on to a floured surface and roll out to a rectangle, approximately 30 × 25 cm (12 × 10 inches). Make the edges slightly thicker than the centre. Put the dough on an oiled baking sheet.

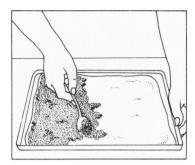

4 Mash the tomatoes with half of their juice so that there are no large lumps, then spread them evenly over the dough, right to the edges. Sprinkle with salt and pepper to taste.

5 Arrange the slices of Mozzarella over the tomatoes, then sprinkle over the strips of ham. Top with the mushrooms and mussels or anchovies, then dot with the olives.

6 Mix together the oregano and remaining oil, and add salt and pepper to taste. Drizzle over the top of the pizza.

7 Leave the pizza to prove in a warm place for about 30 minutes, then bake in the oven at 220°C (425°F) mark 7 for 25 minutes or until the topping is melted and the dough well risen. Cut into serving portions and serve hot or cold.

Menu Suggestion
Serve for a family supper with a crisp green salad of lettuce, chicory or endive and fennel.

PIZZETTE FRITTE
(PAN-FRIED MINI PIZZAS)

1.15*	215 cals

* plus 1½–2 hours rising

Makes 12

1 quantity of basic pizza dough
(see page 149)

30 ml (2 tbsp) olive oil

1 small onion, skinned and finely
chopped

1–2 garlic cloves, skinned and
crushed

350 g (12 oz) ripe tomatoes,
skinned and roughly chopped,
or 397 g (14 oz) can tomatoes

20 ml (4 tsp) chopped fresh basil or
10 ml (2 tsp) dried

pinch of sugar, or to taste

salt and freshly ground pepper

vegetable oil, for shallow frying

1 Make the basic pizza dough
according to the instructions
on page 149 and leave to rise.

2 Heat the olive oil in a pan, add
the onion and garlic and fry
gently for 5 minutes until soft and
lightly coloured. Add the tomatoes
and break them up with a spoon.
Bring to the boil, then lower the
heat, add the basil, sugar and salt
and pepper to taste. Simmer for
about 20 minutes, stirring
frequently.

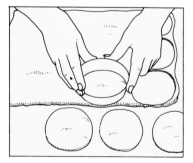

3 Meanwhile, turn the risen
dough out on to a floured surface, roll out and cut into twelve
10-cm (4-inch) circles.

4 Work the tomato mixture in a
blender or food processor.
Return to the rinsed-out pan, taste
and adjust seasoning, then reheat
gently while frying the pizzas.

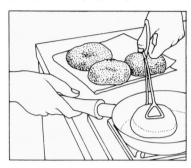

5 Heat the vegetable oil in a
small frying pan and shallow
fry the pizzas in batches for about
2 minutes on each side until they
are golden.

6 Drain the pizzas quickly on
absorbent kitchen paper, then
spread with some of the sauce.
Serve immediately.

Menu Suggestion
Serve as a snack on their own, at
any time of day.

PIZZETTE FRITTE
This is just one of the many
versions of pizza, which
originated in Naples and is now
found all over the world. The
original pizza had a simple topping of tomatoes, anchovies and
cheese, but nowadays pizzerie
specialise in the most fanciful of
toppings. Pizzette Fritte make an
ideal snack, because they are
small enough to be eaten with
the fingers.

PANZEROTTI
(DEEP-FRIED STUFFED PIZZAS)

1.00* £ ✳* 173 cals

* plus 1½–2 hours rising; freeze after
step 7

Makes 16

**1 quantity of basic pizza dough
(see page 149)**

**300 ml (½ pint) Salsa di Pomodoro
(see page 144)**

**100 g (4 oz) Italian Mozzarella
cheese**

**25 g (1 oz) freshly grated Parmesan
cheese**

50 g (2 oz) boiled ham, finely diced

salt and freshly ground pepper

vegetable oil, for deep frying

1 Make the basic pizza dough
according to the instructions
on page 149 and leave to rise.

2 Cook the tomato sauce, over
high heat, stirring constantly,
until reduced to a thick pulp.
Leave to cool for about 30
minutes.

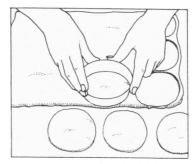

3 Meanwhile, turn the risen
dough out on to a floured
surface, roll out and cut into sixteen 10-cm (4-inch) circles. Use a
plain pastry cutter or the rim of a
wine glass or cup as a guide.

4 Spread the cold tomato sauce
over the circles of dough,
leaving a border at the edge.

5 Roughly chop the Mozzarella.
Mix it with Parmesan, ham and
seasoning. Sprinkle over one half
of dough.

6 Brush the edge of the dough
with water, then fold the plain
half over the filled half.

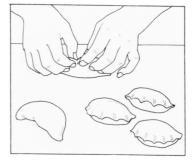

7 Press the edges of the
panzerotti together well to seal
in the filling, then crimp to make
a decorative edge.

8 Heat the oil in a deep-fat frier
to 180°C (350°F). Deep-fry
the pizzas in batches for 2–3
minutes on both sides until golden.
Drain and serve immediately.

Menu Suggestion
Serve hot as a snack on their own,
or cold as part of a picnic or al
fresco buffet.

Cheese and Eggs

Both cheese and eggs are used extensively in Italian cookery—with these two ingredients in the kitchen, it seems an Italian cook can always get together a delicious dish with the minimum of effort and very little expense. Most cheese and egg dishes are served for the evening meal in Italy, because for the majority of families the main meal of the day is at lunchtime. Light and easily digested, the recipes in this chapter are suitable for lunch or supper, whichever you prefer.

FRITTATA
(ITALIAN OMELETTE)

| 0.20 | 408 cals |

Serves 4

6 eggs

30 ml (2 tbsp) freshly grated Parmesan cheese

salt and freshly ground pepper

25 g (1 oz) butter

15 ml (1 tbsp) olive oil

100 g (4 oz) Mortadella sausage, cut into thin strips

100 g (4 oz) Italian Mozzarella cheese, cut into thin slices

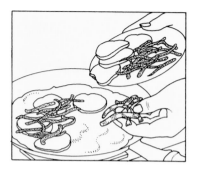

1 Beat the eggs together in a bowl. Add the freshly grated Parmesan cheese and salt and pepper to taste.

2 Melt the butter with the oil in a large, heavy-based frying pan and, when hot, add the eggs. Cook gently for about 5–8 minutes until the mixture is half set underneath and the top of the omelette is still runny.

3 Scatter the Mortadella and Mozzarella over the omelette, then cook for 5 minutes until eggs are set.

4 Place pan under heated grill for 2–3 minutes until top of omelette is set. Serve hot, cut into wedges.

Menu Suggestion
Serve for a light lunch with a mixed salad and fresh bread.

VARIATIONS

Omit the Mortadella and Mozzarella, then add one of the following variations.
Vegetable omelette: Fry 1 seeded and finely sliced red pepper in olive oil and butter until lightly coloured. Add 2 thinly sliced courgettes and 2 skinned and roughly chopped tomatoes and cook for 10 minutes until slightly reduced and thickened. Spread this onto omelette after step 2 and cook as above.

Onion omelette: Heat 30 ml (2 tbsp) olive oil in a frying pan, slowly cook 3 finely sliced large onions over low heat until soft and golden. Add this to beaten eggs and cook as above.
Salami omelette: Scatter 100 g (4 oz) diced salami over the omelette at step 3.
Cheese omelette: Add 100 g (4 oz) freshly grated Parmesan cheese to the beaten egg mixture and cook as above.

TIMBALLO DI RISO
(RICE MOULD WITH CHEESE, MUSHROOMS AND EGGS)

| 2.00 | 537 cals |

Serves 8

75 g (3 oz) butter

1 onion, skinned and finely chopped

400 g (14 oz) arborio rice (see page 132)

180 ml (12 tbsp) dry white wine

about 1.2 litres (2 pints) hot chicken stock (see page 148)

salt and freshly ground pepper

30 ml (2 tbsp) olive oil

225 g (8 oz) mushrooms, sliced

2 garlic cloves, skinned and crushed

10 ml (2 tsp) chopped fresh basil or 5 ml (1 tsp) dried

60 ml (4 tbsp) dried breadcrumbs

50 g (2 oz) freshly grated Parmesan cheese

2 eggs, beaten

3 hard-boiled eggs, shelled and sliced

225 g (8 oz) Italian Mozzarella cheese, sliced

300 ml (½ pint) Salsa di Pomodoro, to serve (see page 144)

1 Make a risotto. Melt 50 g (2 oz) of the butter in a heavy-based saucepan. Add the onion and fry gently for 5 minutes until soft but not coloured.

2 Add the rice and stir until coated in the butter, then pour in 150 ml (¼ pint) of the wine and bring to the boil. Simmer, stirring, until the rice has absorbed all the cooking liquid.

3 Pour in about 150 ml (¼ pint) of stock, add 5 ml (1 tsp) salt and simmer and stir as before until all the liquid is absorbed. Continue adding stock in this way until the rice is just tender; this should take 15–20 minutes.

4 Meanwhile, heat the oil in a separate pan, add the mushrooms and garlic and fry gently until the juices run. Stir in the remaining wine, the basil and seasoning to taste. Remove from the heat.

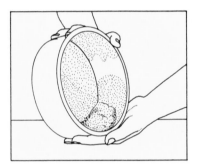

5 Sprinkle the breadcrumbs over the base and up the sides of a well-buttered 20-cm (8-inch) spring-release cake tin or mould, making sure there are no gaps.

6 Remove the risotto from the heat and stir in the Parmesan cheese with the beaten eggs, the remaining butter and salt and pepper to taste.

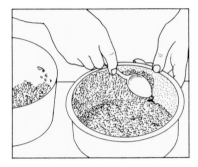

7 Press three-quarters of the risotto over the base and up the sides of the lined tin. Arrange about one-third of the hard-boiled egg slices in the bottom, then sprinkle over about one-third of the mushrooms. Top with one-third of the Mozzarella slices.

8 Repeat these layers until all the eggs, mushrooms and Mozzarella are used up, then press the remaining risotto firmly on top.

9 Cover the tin with foil and bake in the oven at 190°C (375°F) mark 5 for 1 hour until firm. Leave to rest in the tin for 5 minutes, then turn out on to a warmed serving platter. Serve immediately, with tomato sauce handed separately.

Menu Suggestion
Serve for a lunch or supper dish with a salad of fennel and tomatoes tossed in a dressing of olive oil, lemon juice and chopped fresh basil.

TIMBALLO DI RISO
Timballo comes from the region around Naples, and there are many different versions. The basic risotto mixture which forms the case for the filling is usually the same, but the filling varies from one cook and one occasion to another—you literally fill your timballo with whatever you have to hand! Sweetbreads, chicken livers, chopped bacon and even small spicy sausages can be used to fill the centre of a timballo, and the tomato sauce for serving suggested here can be changed to a cream, cheese or meat sauce, whichever complements the filling best.

MOZZARELLA IN CARROZZA
(DEEP-FRIED MOZZARELLA SANDWICHES)

| 0.20 | 🍴 | 268 cals |

Makes 10

175 g (6 oz) Italian Mozzarella
  cheese

10 large slices of white bread,
  crusts removed

salt and freshly ground pepper

2 eggs

175 ml (6 fl oz) milk

75 g (3 oz) plain flour

vegetable oil, for frying

1 Slice the cheese thinly and
arrange on five slices of bread,
leaving a narrow margin around
the edges. Season with salt and
pepper and cover with the remaining bread slices. Cut each sandwich in half diagonally or
widthways.

2 Beat the eggs in a shallow bowl
and add the milk. Season
generously with salt and pepper.
Spread flour out on a flat plate.

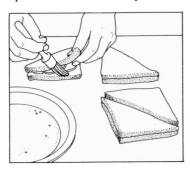

3 Brush a little egg and milk
mixture inside edges of sandwiches and press together.

4 Quickly dip each sandwich
into the egg mixture, then
coat lightly with the flour. Dip
again into the egg mixture,
shaking off any excess.

5 Pour enough oil into a frying
pan to come 1 cm (½ inch) up
the sides of the pan and heat until
it is hot.

6 Carefully place the sandwiches
in the pan, in a single layer. (If
your pan is not large enough you
may have to use two pans or cook
the sandwiches in batches.) Fry
for about 3 minutes on each side
until brown. Drain on absorbent
kitchen paper and serve
immediately.

Menu Suggestion
Serve hot as a snack on their own,
or as a starter before a light main
course.

MELANZANE RIPIENE AL FORMAGGIO
(STUFFED AUBERGINES)

1.45	454 cals

Serves 4

4 small aubergines

salt and freshly ground pepper

30 ml (2 tbsp) olive oil

25 g (1 oz) butter

1 small onion, skinned and very finely chopped

4 small ripe tomatoes, skinned and roughly chopped

10 ml (2 tsp) chopped fresh basil or 5 ml (1 tsp) dried

2 hard-boiled eggs, shelled and roughly chopped

15 ml (1 tbsp) capers

225 g (8 oz) Fontina cheese, sliced

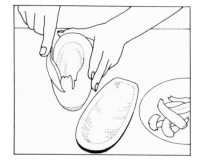

1 Wash and dry the aubergines. Cut each one in half lengthways and scoop out the flesh.

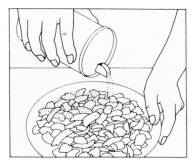

2 Chop the flesh finely, then spread out on a plate and sprinkle with salt. Leave for 20 minutes to remove bitter flavour. Turn aubergine flesh into a colander. Rinse, drain and dry.

3 Heat half of the oil in a pan with the butter, add the onion and fry gently for 5 minutes until soft but not coloured. Add the aubergine flesh, the tomatoes, basil and seasoning to taste.

4 Meanwhile, put the aubergines in a single layer in an oiled ovenproof dish. Brush the insides with the remaining oil, then bake in the oven at 180°C (350°F) mark 4 for 10 minutes.

5 Spoon half of the tomato mixture into the base of the aubergine shells. Cover with a layer of chopped eggs, capers, then with a layer of cheese. Spoon the remaining tomato mixture over the top. Return to the oven and bake for a further 15 minutes until sizzling hot. Serve immediately.

Menu Suggestion

Serve as a lunch or supper dish with fresh bread and a red wine such as Chianti Classico.

CRESPELLE
(PANCAKES STUFFED WITH CHEESE AND SPINACH)

| 1.00 | ✳* | 788 cals |

* freeze after step 8

Serves 4

450 g (1 lb) washed fresh spinach or 226 g (8 oz) packet frozen spinach

50 g (2 oz) butter

1 small onion, skinned and finely chopped

65 g (2½ oz) freshly grated Parmesan cheese

600 ml (1 pint) béchamel sauce (see page 148)

salt and freshly ground pepper

100 g (4 oz) plain flour

1 egg

300 ml (½ pint) milk

oil, for frying

1 Make the filling. Place the spinach in a saucepan without any water and cook gently for 5–10 minutes (or until thawed if using frozen spinach). Drain well and chop finely.

2 Melt the 50 g (2 oz) butter in a saucepan, add the onion and fry gently for 5 minutes until soft but not coloured. Stir in the spinach and cook for a further 2 minutes. Remove from the heat and stir in 50 g (2 oz) Parmesan cheese, 90 ml (6 tbsp) béchamel sauce and seasoning to taste.

3 Make the batter. Place the flour and a pinch of salt in a bowl. Make a well in the centre and add the egg. Beat well with a wooden spoon and gradually beat in the milk.

4 Cook the pancakes. Heat a little oil in an 18-cm (7-inch) heavy-based frying pan until hot, running it round the base and sides of the pan. Pour off any surplus.

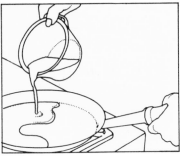

5 Pour in just enough batter to coat the base of pan thinly. Fry for 1–2 minutes until golden brown, turn or toss and cook the second side until golden.

6 Transfer the pancake to a plate. Repeat with the remaining batter to make eight pancakes. Pile the cooked pancakes on top of each other with greaseproof paper in between each one.

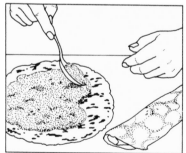

7 Spread an equal amount of the filling on each pancake, leaving a border around the edge. Roll up the pancakes loosely.

8 Arrange the pancakes in a single layer in a buttered oven-proof dish, then pour over the remaining béchamel sauce and sprinkle with the remaining Parmesan cheese.

9 Bake in the oven at 220°C (425°F) mark 7 for about 10 minutes until golden brown. Serve the pancakes hot.

Menu Suggestion
Serve as a first course for a dinner party, with Pollo alla Diavola (page 92) to follow and fresh fruit to finish.

CRESPELLE
Crespelle, sometimes called crespellini, are similar to cannelloni in appearance except that they are made from a pancake batter rather than a pasta dough. Fillings can be as varied as those for cannelloni, so there is no reason to stick to this recipe for cheese and spinach, which comes from Florence. Minced beef, tomato, herbs and garlic would make a tasty alternative filling, so too would minced chicken and béchamel sauce flavoured with freshly grated nutmeg.

POLENTA FRITTA
(FRIED POLENTA STICKS)

0.45*	🍴	570 cals*

* plus 1 hour cooling; 690 cals if using
350 g (12 oz) cheese

Serves 4

1 litre (1¾ pints) water

10 ml (2 tsp) salt

225 g (8 oz) coarse-grain cornmeal
   or polenta flour

vegetable oil, for frying

250–350 g (8–12 oz) Torta San
   Gaudenzio or Fontina cheese

Salsa di Pomodoro (see page 144)

1 Make the polenta sticks. Put
the water and salt in a large
pan and bring to simmering point.

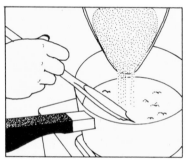

2 Add the cornmeal in a very
fine stream, stirring vigorously
all the time with a long-handled
wooden spoon. Do not add the
cornmeal all at once or it will become hard.

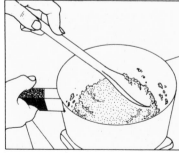

3 When the mixture is smooth
and thick, simmer for 20–30
minutes, stirring, until polenta
comes away from sides of pan.

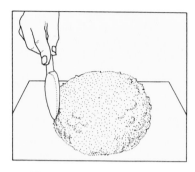

4 Turn on to a wooden board
and shape it into a cake about
5 cm (2 inches) high with a
dampened wooden spoon. Leave
for about 1 hour to cool.

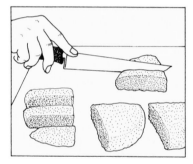

5 When cold, divide the polenta
into four sections, then cut
each of the sections into 2.5-cm
(1-inch) sticks.

6 Heat enough oil in a frying
pan to come 2.5 cm (1 inch) up
the sides of the pan. Fry the
polenta sticks in batches for about
3 minutes on each side until crisp.
Drain on absorbent kitchen paper
and serve hot, with slices of the
cheese and the tomato sauce
handed separately.

Menu Suggestion
Serve for an informal lunch or
supper dish with a full-bodied red
wine. Follow with a green salad.

ROTOLO DI SPINACI *(SPINACH ROLL)*

| 1.20* | 🍴 | ✳* | 653 cals |

* plus 2 hours cooling; freeze after step 11

Serves 8

450 g (1 lb) old potatoes, peeled
salt and freshly ground pepper
900 g (2 lb) washed fresh spinach or 450 g (1 lb) packet frozen spinach
30 ml (2 tbsp) olive oil
1 onion, skinned and chopped
100 g (4 oz) curd cheese
50 g (2 oz) Italian salami, finely chopped
50 g (2 oz) freshly grated Parmesan cheese
pinch of freshly grated nutmeg
2 eggs
5 ml (1 tsp) baking powder
about 200 g (7 oz) plain flour
50 g (2 oz) butter
Salsa di Pomodoro alla Napoletana, to serve (see page 145)

1 Cook the potatoes in a saucepan of boiling salted water for about 20 minutes until tender.

2 Meanwhile, prepare the filling. Place the spinach in a saucepan without any water and cook gently for 5–10 minutes (or until thawed if using frozen spinach). Drain well and chop finely.

3 Heat the oil in a frying pan, add the onion and fry gently for 2–3 minutes until soft but not coloured. Add the spinach and cook for a further 2 minutes.

4 Turn the spinach into a bowl and add the curd cheese, salami, 25 g (1 oz) Parmesan cheese, nutmeg, 1 egg and seasoning. Beat well together.

5 Drain cooked potatoes, then push them through a sieve into a bowl. Make a well in the centre and add the remaining egg, the baking powder and most of the flour. Beat well together.

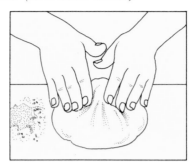

6 Knead on a work surface, adding more flour if necessary, for about 5 minutes. The dough should be smooth and slightly sticky. Shape dough into a ball.

7 Roll out the dough to a rectangle about 35.5 × 30.5 cm (14 × 12 inches). Spread the spinach mixture over the dough, leaving a 2.5 cm (1 inch) border.

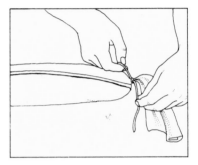

8 Roll the dough into a sausage shape. Wrap tightly in a muslin cloth. Tie ends with string.

9 Bring a large flameproof casserole, roasting tin or fish kettle of salted water to the boil and place the roll in it. Return to the boil then simmer, partially covered, for 30 minutes. Remove the roll from the water, unwrap and leave to cool for 2 hours.

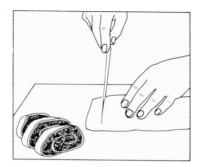

10 Cut the roll into 2.5-cm (1-inch) thick slices and arrange the slices, slightly overlapping, in an ovenproof dish.

11 Melt the butter and pour over the slices. Sprinkle with the remaining Parmesan cheese and bake in the oven at 200°C (400°F) mark 6 for about 15 minutes until golden. Serve hot, with tomato sauce handed separately.

Menu Suggestion
Serve this substantial dish for lunch, with a chilled dry white wine such as Frascati.

Main Courses

Italian main courses are
invariably light and
simple. On the whole,
meals are lengthy with
several courses, therefore
the main course is not
quite so important or
substantial as it is in
other cuisines. Simple
dishes of grilled or roast
meat and poultry, fried
escalopes and charcoal-
grilled fish are preferred.
Sauces should be light
and subtle in order not to
disguise the flavour of the
food they are served with.
An Italian cook takes
great pride in choosing
ingredients—it's the
quality that counts, not
the quantity.

SCAMPI FRITTI
*(PRAWNS FRIED
IN GARLIC)*

| 0.07 | £ £ | 477 cals |

Serves 2

50 g (2 oz) butter

30 ml (2 tbsp) olive oil

12 unshelled jumbo prawns

3 garlic cloves, skinned and
  crushed

60 ml (4 tbsp) brandy

salt and freshly ground pepper

lemon wedges and shredded
  lettuce, to serve

1 Melt the butter with the oil in
a large, heavy-based pan. Add
the prawns (cook half at a time if
your pan is not large enough)
and the garlic and fry over high
heat for 5 minutes, tossing the
prawns constantly.

2 Sprinkle the brandy over the
prawns with salt and pepper to
taste. Serve immediately,
garnished with lemon and lettuce.

Menu Suggestion
Serve for a light luncheon with a
chilled dry white wine. Follow
with Crocchette di Patate (page
97) served with a simple tomato
sauce (page 144), then finish with
Insalata di Finocchi e Cetrioli
(page 109).

SCAMPI FRITTI

In Italy the giant scampi used
for this dish are caught in
Mediterranean waters and are
relatively easy to come by. The
nearest equivalent in size is the
Dublin Bay Prawn, which is only
available at specialist fishmongers and is very expensive.
You can use smaller prawns if
you wish, but the dish will lose
its spectacular looks!

TRIGLIE AL CARTOCCIO
(RED MULLET PARCELS)

| 0.45 | ✳* | 378 cals |

* freeze after step 5

Serves 4

60 ml (4 tbsp) olive oil

60 ml (4 tbsp) dry white vermouth

2 garlic cloves, skinned and
   crushed

salt and freshly ground pepper

4 red mullet, each weighing about
   225 g (8 oz), cleaned

4 sprigs of rosemary

fresh rosemary sprigs and lemon
   slices, to garnish

1 Mix together the oil, vermouth
and garlic. Add salt and
pepper to taste.

2 Cut four rectangles of foil,
each one large enough to en-
close one red mullet. Brush with a
little of the olive oil mixture.

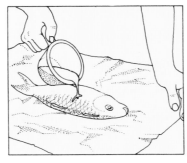

3 Place one fish in the centre of
each piece of foil and pour
over the remaining olive oil mixture. Place a rosemary sprig on top
of each fish.

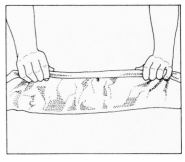

4 Bring the long sides of the foil
to meet over the fish and fold
over several times to close and
seal completely.

5 Fold over the ends of the foil
so that the fish are completely
sealed in, as if in a parcel.

6 Put the parcels in a single layer
in a baking tin and bake in the
oven at 180°C (350°F) mark 4 for
20 minutes or until tender.

7 To serve. Remove the fish
from the parcels and place on a
warmed serving dish. Pour over
the juices that have collected on
the foil. Garnish each fish with a
fresh rosemary sprig and a slice of
lemon and serve immediately.

Menu Suggestion
Start the meal with Pomodori
Ripieni alla Mozzarella (page 105)
and finish with Zuccotto
(page 114).

SOGLIOLE AL MARSALA
(PAN-FRIED SOLE WITH MARSALA)

| 0.15 | £ £ | 349 cals |

Serves 4

8 sole quarter-cut fillets (two from each side of fish)

plain flour

salt and freshly ground pepper

75 g (3 oz) butter

120 ml (8 tbsp) dry Marsala

120 ml (8 tbsp) double cream

chopped fresh parsley and lemon wedges, to garnish

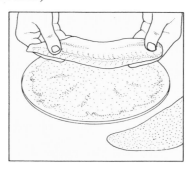

1 Dip each of the eight sole fillets in the flour seasoned with salt and pepper. Coat both sides of the fish evenly, shaking off any excess.

2 Melt the butter in two large frying pans and fry the fish, all at once, for 2–3 minutes on each side until just cooked.

3 Sprinkle over the Marsala and cream, then add salt and pepper to taste. Shake the pans and let the sauce bubble for 2 minutes.

4 Serve immediately, garnished with chopped parsley, and lemon wedges.

Menu Suggestion
Serve Antipasto Misto (page 16) to start and finish with Torta di Mele (page 123).

BISTECCHE ALLA PIZZAIOLA
(RUMP STEAKS WITH TOMATO, GARLIC AND OLIVE SAUCE)

0.30	£ £	407 cals

Serves 4

30 ml (2 tbsp) olive oil, plus extra
   for frying

2–3 garlic cloves, skinned and
   sliced

700 g (1½ lb) ripe tomatoes, skinned
   and roughly chopped, or two
   397 g (14 oz) cans tomatoes,
   drained

15 ml (1 tbsp) chopped fresh
   oregano or basil, or 5 ml (1 tsp)
   dried

salt and freshly ground pepper

four 175 g (6 oz) rump steaks,
   trimmed

100 g (4 oz) large black olives

1 Make the sauce. Heat the oil in a medium saucepan, add the sliced garlic and cook gently for about 1 minute.

2 Add the tomatoes with the herbs and salt and pepper to taste. Boil gently for 15 minutes, until the tomatoes have cooked down but have not completely disintegrated.

3 Heat a little olive oil in a large frying pan. Fry the steaks for 2 minutes on each side.

4 Meanwhile, stone the olives and roughly chop the flesh. Coat steaks with sauce, add olives and cook, covered, for 5 minutes.

Menu Suggestion
Start with Uove Tonnate (page 22) and finish with fresh fruit.

MANZO STUFATO AL VINO ROSSO
(BEEF STEWED IN RED WINE)

3.45*	✳*	441 cals

* plus 4–5 hours marinating; freeze after step 2

Serves 6

1.4 kg (3 lb) piece top rump or chuck steak, trimmed

450 ml ($\frac{3}{4}$ pint) red wine

1 onion, skinned and finely sliced

3 garlic cloves, skinned and sliced

3 parsley stalks, lightly crushed

8 peppercorns

sprig of fresh thyme or 2.5 ml ($\frac{1}{2}$ tsp) dried

30 ml (2 tbsp) olive oil

about 150 ml ($\frac{1}{4}$ pint) beef stock

100 g (4 oz) lean gammon, cut into cubes

salt and freshly ground pepper

1 Place the piece of beef in a plastic bag or bowl, pour in the wine and add the onion, garlic, parsley stalks, peppercorns and thyme. Mix well to combine. Alternatively, the beef can be cut into large pieces first.

2 Seal the bag or cover the bowl and leave in a cool place to marinate for 4–5 hours.

3 Remove the beef from the marinade. Set aside. Strain the marinade and set aside. Reserve the onion slices.

4 Heat the oil in a heavy flame-proof casserole, add the reserved onion slices and fry gently for 5 minutes until soft but not coloured. Add the beef and fry it for about 10 minutes until brown on all sides.

5 Pour over the marinade and the 150 ml ($\frac{1}{4}$ pint) stock, then add the cubes of gammon. Season with salt and pepper. Bring to the boil and boil rapidly for about 2–3 minutes.

6 Cover tightly and cook in the oven at 180°C (350°F) mark 4 for 2$\frac{1}{2}$–3 hours until the beef is tender. Check every 30 minutes, turning the beef and making sure that the liquid has not evaporated. If necessary, top up with a little stock or water.

7 To serve, remove the cooked beef from the casserole and slice neatly. Arrange the slices overlapping on a warmed serving platter. Taste and adjust the seasoning of the sauce, then serve immediately, with the sliced beef.

Menu Suggestion
Serve Zucchini alla Ricotta (page 101) as a first course.

SCALOPPINE AL LIMONE
(VEAL ESCALOPES WITH LEMON)

0.25	305 cals

Serves 4

4 veal escalopes
30 ml (2 tbsp) plain flour
salt and freshly ground pepper
50 g (2 oz) butter
60 ml (4 tbsp) olive oil
45 ml (3 tbsp) lemon juice
90 ml (6 tbsp) dry white wine
lemon slices and sprigs of Italian or continental parsley, to garnish

1 Put the escalopes between two sheets of greaseproof paper and bat out until thin with a meat mallet or rolling pin.

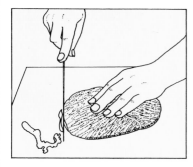

2 Trim the escalopes to size, then coat in the flour seasoned with salt and pepper. Make sure both sides are evenly coated.

3 Melt the butter with the oil in a large, heavy-based frying pan. Add the escalopes and fry for 3–4 minutes on each side until tender. (If you do not have a pan large enough to cook all four escalopes together, either use two frying pans or cook two first and then keep them warm while you are cooking the others.)

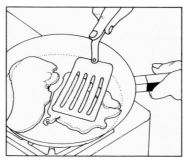

4 During cooking, press the escalopes constantly with a fish slice to help prevent shrinkage and keep them as flat as possible.

5 Transfer the escalopes to a warmed serving platter with a fish slice, cover and keep warm.

6 Add the lemon juice and wine to the pan and stir to combine with the cooking juices. Bubble vigorously for a minute or two, then add salt and pepper to taste. Pour over the escalopes, garnish with lemon slices and parsley sprigs and serve immediately.

Menu Suggestion
Serve Funghi Ripieni al Forno (page 21) as a starter and finish with Zuppa Inglese (page 120).

OSSO BUCO
(BRAISED VEAL IN WHITE WINE)

| 2.30 | £ | ✳ | 957 cals |

Serves 4

50 g (2 oz) butter

15 ml (1 tbsp) olive oil

1 onion, skinned and finely chopped

4–8 ossi buchi (veal shin, hind cut), sawn into 5 cm (2 inch) lengths, weighing about 1.75 kg (3½ lb)

50 g (2 oz) plain flour

salt and freshly ground pepper

300 ml (½ pint) dry white wine

300 ml (½ pint) veal or chicken stock (see page 148)

finely grated rind of 1 lemon

1 garlic clove, skinned and finely chopped

45 ml (3 tbsp) chopped fresh parsley

Risotto alla Milanese, to serve (see page 50)

1 Melt the butter with the oil in a flameproof casserole, add the onion and fry gently for 5 minutes until soft but not coloured.

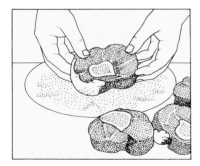

2 Coat the veal in the flour seasoned with salt and pepper. Add to the casserole and fry for about 10 minutes until browned all over.

3 Pour over the wine and boil rapidly for 5 minutes, then add the veal or chicken stock.

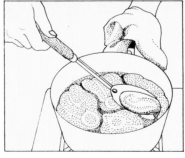

4 Cover the pan tightly and simmer for 1½–2 hours, basting and turning the meat occasionally.

5 When the meat is cooked, transfer to a warmed serving dish, cover and keep warm. If necessary, boil the sauce rapidly to reduce and thicken, then pour over the meat.

6 Mix together the lemon rind, garlic and parsley and sprinkle over the finished dish. Serve hot, with Risotto alla Milanese.

Menu Suggestion
Serve with Insalata di Frutti di Mare (page 24) as a first course and fresh fruit to follow.

OSSO BUCO

This classic dish is from the city of Milan in Lombardy, where it is always garnished, as here, with lemon rind, garlic and parsley, called gremolata in Italian. Be sure to buy the correct cut of veal—the shin or shank. This contains the marrow, considered to be a great delicacy and traditionally dug out of the bones with a silver spoon.

BRACIOLE DI MAIALE
(PORK CHOPS WITH HERBS)

0.50	691 cals

Serves 4

15 ml (1 tbsp) plain flour

5 ml (1 tsp) chopped fresh sage or
   2.5 ml ($\frac{1}{2}$ tsp) dried

5 ml (1 tsp) chopped fresh
   marjoram or 2.5 ml (1 tsp) dried

salt and freshly ground pepper

4 pork loin chops, trimmed of
   excess fat

30 ml (2 tbsp) olive oil

15 g ($\frac{1}{2}$ oz) butter

300 ml ($\frac{1}{2}$ pint) Salsa di Pomodoro
   (see page 144)

350 g (12 oz) spaghetti or other long
   thin pasta (see pages 130–131),
   to serve

fresh sage and marjoram sprigs,
   to garnish

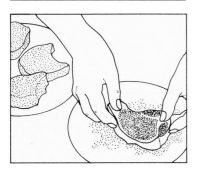

1 On a flat plate, mix together the flour and herbs with a liberal sprinkling of salt and pepper. Coat the chops in the flour mixture.

2 Heat the oil with the butter in a heavy-based frying pan. Add the chops and fry over moderate heat for a few minutes on each side until golden.

3 Pour the tomato sauce into the base of an ovenproof serving dish. Transfer the chops to the serving dish.

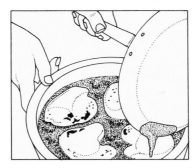

4 Pour over the cooking juices from the frying pan. Cover the dish with a lid or foil and bake in the oven at 180°C (350°F) mark 4 for 30 minutes.

5 Meanwhile, cook the spaghetti in boiling salted water for 8–12 minutes until just tender.

6 Drain the spaghetti well. To serve, arrange the chops at one end of the serving dish and garnish with the sprigs of herbs. Arrange the spaghetti at the other end. Serve immediately.

Menu Suggestion
Serve for a family meal followed by a crisp green salad and some fresh fruit.

BRACIOLE DI MAIALE
This tasty dish of pork chops served with spaghetti and tomato sauce would be served differently in Italy. The spaghetti and tomato sauce would be eaten separately as a first course, then the chops would follow on their own, with maybe a green or mixed salad to refresh the palate afterwards. Italians never eat the pasta and meat course together, but it is a matter of personal preference how you serve them.

FEGATO ALLA VENEZIANA
(CALF'S LIVER WITH ONIONS AND SAGE)

| 0.35 | 285 cals |

Serves 6

50 g (2 oz) butter

45 ml (3 tbsp) olive or vegetable oil

2 large onions, skinned and sliced

6 fresh sage leaves

12 slices of calf's liver

salt and freshly ground pepper

15 ml (1 tbsp) white wine vinegar

fresh sage leaves and lemon
    wedges, to garnish

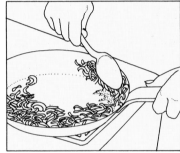

1 Heat the butter and oil in a frying pan. Add the onions and cook very gently for 20 minutes, stirring occasionally, until soft. Stir in sage and cook for 2–3 minutes.

2 Add the liver to the pan. Raise heat and fry for 2–3 minutes on each side.

3 Season the liver, then transfer to a warmed serving dish with the onions. Cover and keep hot. Add the vinegar to the pan and boil briskly for 1–2 minutes, stirring in sediment from pan.

4 To serve. Pour the vinegar mixture over the liver and garnish with sage and lemon.

Menu Suggestion
Serve for an informal supper followed by Crocchette di Patate (page 97).

Abbachio alla Romana
(ROAST LAMB ROMAN-STYLE)

| 2.20 | 310–465 cals |

Serves 4–6

30 ml (2 tbsp) olive oil

1.4 kg (3 lb) leg of lamb

50 g (2 oz) can anchovy fillets

2 garlic cloves, skinned and crushed

10 ml (2 tsp) chopped fresh rosemary or 5 ml (1 tsp) dried

30 ml (2 tbsp) wine vinegar

salt and freshly ground pepper

150 ml ($\frac{1}{4}$ pint) dry white wine

1 Heat the olive oil in a flame-proof casserole, add the lamb and fry over moderate heat for about 10 minutes until browned and sealed on all sides. Remove from the casserole and leave to cool for about 30 minutes.

2 Meanwhile, make the anchovy paste. Crush the anchovies with their oil in a mortar and pestle. Add the garlic, rosemary and wine vinegar and mix to a smooth paste.

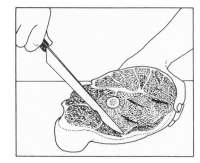

3 Make random incisions all over the leg of lamb with a sharp, pointed knife.

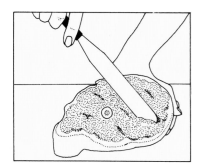

5 Return the lamb to the casserole and roast in the oven at 220°C (425°F) mark 7 for 15 minutes. Lower the oven temperature to 180°C (350°F) mark 4 and roast for a further 1½ hours or until the juices run clear when the thickest part of the meat is pierced with a skewer.

6 Transfer the lamb to a warmed serving platter and keep warm. To serve. Pour the wine into the casserole and stir to dislodge the sediment. Bring to the boil, then simmer, stirring, until the sauce reduces slightly. Serve the lamb carved into slices, with the sauce handed separately.

Menu Suggestion
Serve for Sunday lunch with Stracciatella (page 10) to start and Zuppa Inglese (page 120) to finish.

4 Spread the anchovy paste all over the lamb, working it into the incisions as much as possible. Sprinkle with salt and pepper.

POLLO ALLA VALDOSTANA
(CHICKEN WITH PARMA HAM AND CHEESE)

0.45	£	409 cals

Serves 4

4 boneless chicken breasts, skinned

4 slices of Parma ham or other type of prosciutto (see page 133)

15 ml (1 tbsp) plain flour

5 ml (1 tsp) dried mixed herbs

salt and freshly ground pepper

30 ml (2 tbsp) olive oil

25 g (1 oz) butter

100 g (4 oz) Fontina cheese (see page 134), grated

150 ml ($\frac{1}{4}$ pint) dry white or rosé wine

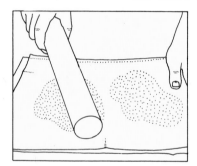

1 Bat the chicken breasts flat with a meat mallet or rolling pin between two sheets of grease-proof paper.

2 Trim the slices of Parma ham to about the same size as the chicken breasts.

3 Put the flour and herbs on a large flat plate, add a liberal sprinkling of salt and pepper and stir well to mix. Coat the chicken pieces on both sides with the flour mixture.

4 Heat the oil with the butter in a large, heavy-based frying pan. Add the chicken pieces and fry over moderate heat for 10 minutes, turning once.

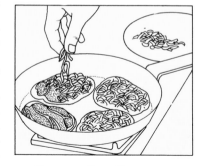

5 Place one slice of ham on top of each chicken breast, then sprinkle the cheese over the top to cover the ham completely.

6 Pour the wine around the chicken and bring to boiling point. Cover the pan tightly, lower the heat to simmering and cook for 5 minutes more until the cheese has melted. Serve hot, with the pan juices poured over the top of the chicken.

Menu Suggestion
Serve Insalata di Funghi (page 108) as a starter and Zuccotto (page 114) for the dessert course. French beans with pine nuts make an interesting vegetable accompaniment to the chicken.

POLLO AL ROSMARINO
(CHICKEN WITH ROSEMARY)

1.00	356 cals

Serves 4

30 ml (2 tbsp) white wine vinegar

7.5 cm (3 inch) sprig of rosemary, chopped

salt and freshly ground pepper

4 chicken leg joints, cut in half

30 ml (2 tbsp) olive oil

lemon wedges, to garnish

1 Put the vinegar into a glass, add 15 ml (1 tbsp) of water, the rosemary and salt and pepper to taste. Stir well, then leave to infuse while cooking the chicken.

2 Season the chicken pieces with salt and pepper. Heat the oil in a large frying pan and, when hot, add the chicken pieces and fry for 5 minutes until they are just golden brown on all sides. Lower the heat and cook uncovered for about 35 minutes.

3 Using two slotted spoons, turn the chicken frequently during cooking until the skin is brown and crisp and the juices run clear when flesh is pierced with a fork.

4 Remove the pan from the heat. When the fat has stopped sizzling, pour over the wine vinegar infusion.

5 Return to the heat, boil rapidly to reduce the liquid for about 5 minutes, then serve immediately, garnished with lemon wedges.

Menu Suggestion
Serve for a family meal accompanied by Crocchette di Patate (page 97) and a simple tomato sauce (page 144). Finish with fresh fruit or a fresh fruit salad.

POLLO ALLA DIAVOLA
(HOT BARBECUED CHICKEN)

0.45* ✳* 474 cals

* plus about 4 hours marinating time; freeze after step 3

Serves 4

8 boneless chicken thighs or 4 chicken portions, skinned

2 garlic cloves, skinned

5 ml (1 tsp) finely chopped dried red chillies (peperoncini)

5 ml (1 tsp) salt

60 ml (4 tbsp) olive oil

juice of $\frac{1}{2}$ lemon

60 ml (4 tbsp) melted butter

lemon wedges, to serve

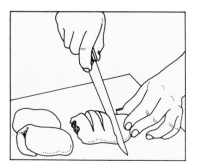

1 Slash the flesh of the chicken thighs or portions, with a sharp, pointed knife.

2 Crush the garlic in a mortar and pestle with the chillies and add salt. Stir in the olive oil and lemon juice until well combined.

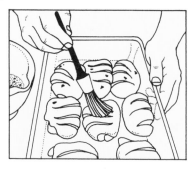

3 Put the chicken in a single layer in a shallow dish. Brush the garlic and chilli mixture over both sides of the chicken, then leave to marinate for 4 hours.

4 Remove the chicken from the dish and place on the oiled grid of a preheated hot barbecue. Cook for about 15 minutes on each side, basting frequently with the melted butter mixed with any remaining marinade from the chicken. (Alternatively, grill under a preheated hot grill for the same amount of time.) Serve hot, with lemon wedges.

Menu Suggestion
Serve as part of a barbecue meal with Peperonata (page 98) or Zucchini in Agrodolce (page 106).

POLLO ALLA DIAVOLA

This simple chicken recipe has many variations, depending on where it originated. For example, Pollo alla Diavola from Tuscany is charcoal-grilled chicken sprinkled with salt, pepper and olive oil and served with slices of lemon. The Tuscan custom is to rub the seasoning and oil into the chicken skin, then to press the bird between two plates, put heavy weights on top and leave for at least 1 hour before cooking. Charcoal grilling is the traditional cooking method, although the bird is also sometimes fried in oil in a deep frying pan and weighted down with a heavy lid during frying. This spicy hot version of Pollo alla Diavola comes from southern Italy, where dried red chillies—peperoncini—are used more extensively than in other regions.

POLLO AL FINOCCHIO
(STUFFED ROAST CHICKEN WITH FENNEL)

2.15	376–564 cals

Serves 4–6

1.8 kg (4 lb) oven-ready chicken
60 ml (4 tbsp) vegetable oil
1 small onion, skinned and finely chopped
1 garlic clove, skinned and crushed
1 small bulb of fennel
4 slices of pancetta (see page 133) or unsmoked streaky bacon, diced
100 g (4 oz) fresh white breadcrumbs
25 g (1 oz) freshly grated Parmesan cheese
1 egg, beaten
salt and freshly ground pepper
25 g (1 oz) butter
150 ml ($\frac{1}{4}$ pint) dry white wine

1 Remove the giblets from the chicken and chop the heart and liver finely. Wash the chicken inside and out, then dry thoroughly.

2 Make the stuffing. Heat half the oil in a small pan, add the onion and garlic and fry gently for 5 minutes until soft but not coloured.

3 Chop the fennel finely, re-serving the feathery tops for the garnish.

4 Add the fennel to the onion and continue frying for 5 minutes, stirring constantly. Add the pancetta and fry 5 minutes more until changing colour.

5 Turn the fried mixture into a bowl. Add the breadcrumbs, Parmesan, egg and salt and pepper to taste. Mix well to combine.

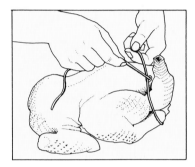

6 Fill the neck end of the chicken with the stuffing, then truss with string.

7 Heat the remaining oil with the butter in a large flame-proof casserole, then brown the chicken lightly on all sides. Turn the right way up, pour in the wine and bring to boiling point. Add salt and pepper to taste.

8 Transfer the casserole to the oven and cook the chicken at 180°C (350°F) mark 4 for $1\frac{3}{4}$ hours, or until the juices run clear when the thickest part of the thigh is pierced with a skewer. Turn the chicken frequently during cooking.

9 To serve. Remove the trussing string and carve the chicken into neat slices. Garnish each serving with a little of the reserved fennel tops. Hand the cooking liquid separately, if liked, or make a gravy in the usual way.

Menu Suggestion
Serve for a family lunch with Budino di Ricotta alla Romana (page 118) for dessert.

Vegetables and Salads

The Italian climate produces such a wealth of wonderful vegetables and salad ingredients, it's small wonder that they play such a large part in the cuisine of the country. From the sun-kissed sweet peppers, tomatoes, aubergines and courgettes of the south, to the more hardy yet equally delicious asparagus, mushrooms, truffles and cardoons of the north, the choice is seemingly endless. Italian cooks serve vegetables and salads as dishes in their own right rather than as accompaniments to main courses, so that their flavour can be appreciated to the full — an idea you might like to follow yourself.

CROCCHETTE DI PATATE
(POTATO AND CHEESE CROQUETTES)

1.00*	✳*	148 cals

* plus 20 minutes cooling and 30 minutes chilling; freeze after step 5

Makes 16

900 g (2 lb) old floury potatoes, peeled

salt and freshly ground pepper

225 g (8 oz) Italian Mozzarella or Provolone cheese, roughly chopped

60 ml (4 tbsp) top of the milk or cream

2 eggs

1.25 ml ($\frac{1}{4}$ tsp) freshly grated nutmeg

plain flour, for coating

25 g (1 oz) freshly grated Parmesan cheese

90 ml (6 tbsp) dried breadcrumbs

vegetable oil, for deep frying

1 Cook the potatoes in boiling salted water for about 20 minutes or until tender. Drain and mash until smooth. Leave to cool for 20–30 minutes.

2 Put the mashed potatoes in a bowl with the Mozzarella or Provolone cheese and milk or cream. Mix well to combine.

3 Add one of the eggs to bind the potato and cheese together, then the nutmeg and salt and pepper to taste. Mix well again.

4 Divide the potato mixture into sixteen. On a floured surface and with floured hands, roll each portion of potato and cheese into a cylinder shape.

5 Beat the remaining egg and use to coat the croquettes. Mix the Parmesan and breadcrumbs together on a flat plate, then roll the croquettes in the mixture until evenly coated. Chill in the refrigerator for at least 30 minutes.

6 Heat the oil in a deep-fat frier to 190°C (375°F). Deep-fry the croquettes in batches for about 3 minutes, turning them so that they become golden brown and crisp on all sides. Drain on absorbent kitchen paper before serving.

Menu Suggestion
Serve as a vegetable accompaniment with a simple tomato sauce (page 144) if liked.

CROCCHETTE DI PATATE

There are two different types of Italian cheese you can use for these croquettes—Mozzarella or Provolone. Both are mild-tasting, with excellent melting qualities. Mozzarella is the more widely available of the two cheeses—it is now made in many countries outside Italy and can be bought in any large super-market. Provolone is more difficult to find and more expen-sive—you will probably have to go to an Italian delicatessen. You may find Provolone sold in a variety of unusual shapes— the shape is in fact immaterial, the cheese inside the waxed outer casing tastes exactly the same, whatever the shape and size.

PEPERONATA
(SWEET PEPPER AND TOMATO STEW)

| 0.45 | £ | ✳ | 156 cals |

Serves 6

75 ml (5 tbsp) olive oil

1 large onion, peeled and finely sliced

6 red peppers, cored, seeded and sliced into strips

2 garlic cloves, skinned and crushed

700 g (1½ lb) ripe tomatoes, skinned and roughly chopped

15 ml (1 tbsp) chopped fresh parsley

salt and freshly ground pepper

1 Heat the oil in a frying pan, add the onion and fry gently for 5 minutes until soft but not coloured.

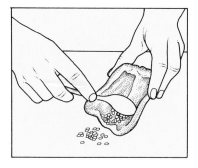

2 Halve the peppers, remove the cores and seeds, then slice the flesh into strips.

3 Add the peppers and garlic, cook gently for 2–3 minutes, then add the tomatoes, parsley and salt and pepper to taste.

4 Cover and cook gently for 30 minutes until the mixture is quite dry: if necessary, remove the lid 10 minutes before the end of cooking and allow the liquid to evaporate. Taste and adjust seasoning before serving either hot or cold.

Menu Suggestion
Serve hot as a vegetable accompaniment to roast, grilled or barbecued meats. Serve cold with chunks of fresh bread for a starter.

POMODORI AL FORNO
(BAKED TOMATOES WITH ANCHOVIES)

0.30	105 cals

Serves 6

3 firm large continental-type tomatoes

1.25 ml ($\frac{1}{4}$ tsp) sugar

freshly ground pepper

30 ml (2 tbsp) olive oil

1 small onion, skinned and very finely chopped

1–2 garlic cloves, skinned and crushed

50 g (2 oz) can anchovy fillets, drained and chopped

20 ml (4 tsp) chopped fresh basil or 10 ml (2 tsp) dried

25 g (1 oz) freshly grated Parmesan cheese

fillets of anchovies, to garnish

1 Cut the tomatoes in half cross-ways. Stand them in an oiled baking dish, levelling the bottoms if necessary so that they will stand upright. Sprinkle with the sugar and pepper. Leave to stand.

2 Heat the oil in a heavy-based pan, add the onion and garlic and fry gently for 5 minutes until soft but not coloured.

3 Add the anchovies and cook for a few minutes more, pressing them with a wooden spoon to break them up.

4 Remove from the heat and stir in the basil, with pepper to taste. (Do not add salt because the anchovies are salty enough.)

5 Spoon the mixture on top of the tomato halves, dividing it equally between them, then sprinkle with the Parmesan.

6 Bake the tomatoes in the oven at 220°C (425°F) mark 7 for 10–15 minutes or until just tender and sizzling. Serve hot, garnished with strips of anchovies.

Menu Suggestion
Serve as a starter with fresh bread rolls, or as a vegetable accompaniment to plain roast or grilled meat.

ZUCCHINI ALLA RICOTTA
(COURGETTES STUFFED WITH RICOTTA)

1.00	232 cals

Serves 4

8 even-sized courgettes

salt and freshly ground pepper

30 ml (2 tbsp) olive oil

1 onion, skinned and finely chopped

1 garlic clove, skinned and crushed

175 g (6 oz) Ricotta cheese

20 ml (4 tsp) chopped fresh basil or 10 ml (2 tsp) dried

300 ml (½ pint) Salsa di Pomodoro (see page 144)

45 ml (3 tbsp) dried breadcrumbs

fresh basil sprigs, to garnish

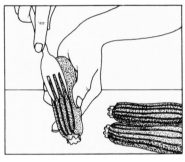

1 Score the courgettes lengthways with the prongs of a fork, then cut them in half lengthways.

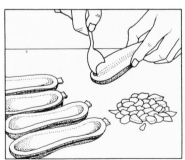

2 Scoop out the flesh from the courgette halves with a sharp-edged teaspoon. Leave a thin margin of flesh next to the skin and make sure not to scoop out all the flesh from the bottoms or the skin may break.

3 Blanch the courgette shells in boiling salted water for 10 minutes. Drain, then stand skin side up on absorbent paper.

4 Heat the oil in a frying pan, add the onion, garlic and scooped-out flesh from the courgettes. Fry gently for about 5 minutes until soft and lightly coloured, then turn into a bowl and add the Ricotta, basil and salt and pepper to taste. Stir well.

5 Spoon the Ricotta filling into the drained courgette shells, dividing it equally between them.

6 Pour the tomato sauce into the bottom of a shallow ovenproof dish which is large enough to hold the courgettes in a single layer. Place the filled courgettes in the dish side by side. Sprinkle with the breadcrumbs.

7 Bake in the oven at 200°C (400°F) mark 6 for 20 minutes. Serve hot, garnished with fresh basil sprigs.

Menu Suggestion
Serve as a first course for a dinner party meal, or as a vegetable accompaniment to a plain main course dish.

FINOCCHI GRATINATI
(FENNEL AU GRATIN)

0.40	234–351 cals

Serves 4–6

4 small bulbs of fennel, trimmed

salt and freshly ground pepper

60 ml (4 tbsp) olive oil

60 ml (4 tbsp) butter

50 g (2 oz) Fontina cheese, grated

**45 ml (3 tbsp) freshly grated
Parmesan cheese**

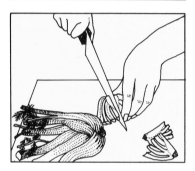

1 Using a sharp knife, carefully cut each bulb of fennel into quarters lengthways.

2 Cook the fennel quarters in a large pan of boiling salted water for 20 minutes until just tender. Drain thoroughly.

3 Heat the oil with the butter in a flameproof gratin dish. Add the fennel and toss to coat in the oil and butter.

4 Turn the fennel quarters cut side up in the dish. Sprinkle with the two cheeses and seasoning.

5 Grill under a preheated hot grill for 5 minutes or until the cheeses are melted and bubbling. Serve hot.

Menu Suggestion
Serve as a vegetable accompaniment; especially good with grilled or barbecued fish.

FINOCCHI GRATINATI
The Fontina cheese in this recipe is a hard, mountain cheese with a sweet, nutty flavour. If difficult to obtain, use Gruyère or Emmental instead.

SPINACI ALLA ROMANA
(SPINACH WITH SULTANAS AND PINE NUTS)

0.30	202 cals

Serves 4

25 g (1 oz) sultanas

**900 g (2 lb) washed fresh spinach or
450 g (1 lb) frozen spinach**

25 g (1 oz) butter

30 ml (2 tbsp) olive oil

1 garlic clove, skinned and crushed

25 g (1 oz) pine nuts

salt and freshly ground pepper

1 Put the sultanas in a bowl, pour in enough hot water to cover and leave to soak for 15 minutes until plump.

2 Place the spinach in a sauce-pan without any water and cook gently for 5–10 minutes, or until thawed if using frozen spinach.

3 Drain the spinach thoroughly and squeeze out as much moisture as possible. Set aside.

4 Melt the butter with the oil in a saucepan, add the garlic and cook gently for 1 minute. Add the spinach and stir until evenly coated with the butter and oil and completely heated through.

5 Drain the sultanas and stir them into the spinach with the pine nuts and salt and pepper to taste. Heat through, then serve immediately to avoid overcooking the spinach.

Menu Suggestion
Serve as a vegetable accom-paniment to any meat or fish dish.

POMODORI RIPIENI ALLA MOZZARELLA
(MOZZARELLA-STUFFED TOMATOES)

0.40*	491 cals

* plus at least 2 hours chilling

Serves 4

4 large, firm tomatoes

salt and freshly ground pepper

50 g (2 oz) black olives

225 g (8 oz) Italian Mozzarella cheese, grated

1–2 garlic cloves, skinned and crushed

20 ml (4 tsp) chopped fresh basil or 10 ml (2 tsp) dried

135 ml (9 tbsp) olive oil

45 ml (3 tbsp) lemon juice

fresh basil sprigs, to garnish

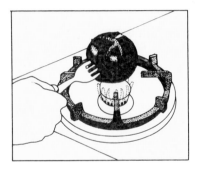

1 Skin the tomatoes. Pierce them one at a time in the stalk end with a fork or skewer and hold over a gas flame or under the grill. Turn the tomato constantly until the skin blisters and bursts, then leave until cool enough to handle. Peel off the skin with your fingers.

2 Cut a slice off the bottom (rounded end) of each tomato. Reserve the slices.

3 Scoop out the insides of the tomatoes with a sharp-edged teaspoon. Sprinkle the insides with salt and stand the tomatoes cut side down to drain on absorbent kitchen paper.

4 Make the stuffing. Reserve four whole black olives, then stone and chop the remainder.

5 Put the Mozzarella in a bowl with the chopped olives, garlic and half the basil. Mix well to combine, then add salt and pepper to taste. (Add salt sparingly because olives tend to be salty.)

6 Place the tomatoes cut side up in a serving dish. Spoon the Mozzarella mixture into the tomatoes, dividing it equally between them. Replace the reserved tomato slices at an angle so that the Mozzarella filling is visible.

7 Whisk together the oil and lemon juice with the remaining basil and salt and pepper to taste. Pour over the tomatoes, then chill in the refrigerator for at least 2 hours, spooning the dressing over from time to time. Serve chilled, garnished with the reserved olives and the basil sprigs.

Menu Suggestion

Serve as a starter with hot bread rolls or garlic bread. Stuffed tomatoes also look good as part of a buffet party spread.

POMODORI RIPIENI ALLA MOZZARELLA

This recipe uses Italian Mozzarella cheese for its soft creamy texture which mixes smoothly with other ingredients. Italian Mozzarella is imported from Italy and also manufactured outside Italy by Italians living abroad—it can be easily identified by its waxed paper wrapping. The cheese inside is moist and fresh, often dripping with whey. Mozzarella made in Scotland or Denmark, which is a harder, waxy cheese, is not suitable for this recipe, although it can be used as a substitute for Mozzarella in recipes such as pizza where it is melted. The best substitute for the Mozzarella in this recipe would be Ricotta or a full-fat soft cheese or cream cheese.

ZUCCHINI IN AGRODOLCE
(COURGETTES IN SWEET-SOUR SAUCE)

0.25	146 cals

Serves 4

450 g (1 lb) small, young courgettes

45 ml (3 tbsp) olive oil

1 small onion, skinned and finely
  chopped

1 garlic clove, skinned and crushed

salt and freshly ground pepper

30 ml (2 tbsp) white wine vinegar

10 ml (2 tsp) sugar

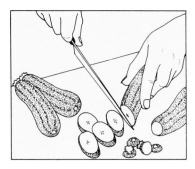

1 Trim the ends off the
courgettes and discard, then
cut the courgettes into thin
diagonal slices.

2 Heat the oil in a large heavy-
based frying pan. Add onion
and garlic and fry for 5 minutes
until soft but not coloured.

3 Add the courgettes and toss to
coat in the oil. Sprinkle with
salt and pepper to taste. Cover pan
and cook gently for 5 minutes
until courgettes are just tender.

4 Mix together the vinegar and
sugar, then pour over the
courgettes. Increase the heat and
toss the courgettes in the cooking
liquid for 1–2 minutes until shiny
and syrupy. Taste and adjust
seasoning before serving.

Menu Suggestion
Serve as a vegetable accompaniment to any meat or fish dish.

INSALATA DI FUNGHI
(MARINATED MUSHROOM SALAD)

0.10*	£	222 cals

* plus 2 hours marinating

Serves 4

90 ml (6 tbsp) olive oil

30 ml (2 tbsp) lemon juice

salt and freshly ground pepper

225 g (8 oz) firm button mushrooms

8 anchovy fillets, soaked in milk (optional)

30 ml (2 tbsp) chopped fresh parsley, to garnish

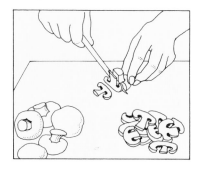

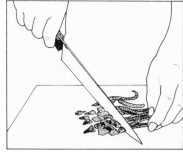

1 Make the dressing. In a medium bowl, mix together the olive oil, lemon juice and freshly ground pepper. (Do not add salt at this stage if you are using anchovies.)

2 Slice the mushrooms finely, then add to the dressing and mix well to coat evenly. Cover and leave to stand in a cool place for at least 2 hours.

3 Just before serving, chop the anchovy fillets, if using, and stir into the mushrooms. Check seasoning and garnish with the chopped parsley.

Menu Suggestion
Serve as a first course dish with herb or hot garlic bread.

INSALATA DI FINOCCHI E CETRIOLI
(FENNEL AND CUCUMBER SALAD)

| 0.35* | 215 cals |

* plus 30 minutes chilling

Serves 4

½ or 1 small cucumber

2 small bulbs of fennel

90 ml (6 tbsp) olive oil

30 ml (2 tbsp) lemon juice

1 garlic clove, skinned and crushed

15 ml (1 tbsp) chopped fresh mint

pinch of sugar

salt and freshly ground pepper

sliced large radishes or tomatoes,
   to serve

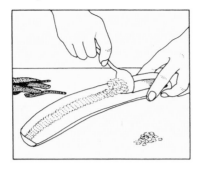

1 Peel the cucumber, then halve lengthways. Scoop out the seeds with a sharp-edged teaspoon and discard. Dice the flesh finely.

2 Trim the fennel, reserving a few feathery tops for the garnish.

3 Grate the fennel into a bowl. Add the diced cucumber and mix together.

4 In a jug, whisk together the remaining ingredients (except the radishes or tomatoes). Add salt and pepper to taste. Pour over the fennel and cucumber and toss well to combine.

5 To serve. Line a shallow serving dish with radish or tomato slices. Taste and adjust the seasoning of the fennel and cucumber salad, then pile in the centre of the dish. Serve chilled, garnished with reserved fennel tops.

Menu Suggestion
Serve this crisp and crunchy salad to refresh the palate after a rich or heavy main course.

INSALATA DI PATATE
(POTATO SALAD)

| 0.20* | 358 cals |

* plus 30 minutes cooling

Serves 4

700 g (1½ lb) waxy potatoes, scrubbed not peeled

90 ml (6 tbsp) olive oil

30 ml (2 tbsp) lemon juice

5 ml (1 tsp) anchovy essence

1 small onion, skinned and finely chopped

1 garlic clove, skinned and crushed

15 ml (1 tbsp) capers, chopped

8 anchovy fillets, soaked in milk and finely chopped (optional)

salt and freshly ground pepper

anchovy fillets, to garnish

1 Cook the potatoes gently in their skins in boiling salted water for about 15 minutes, or until just tender.

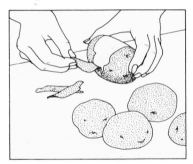

2 Drain the potatoes and leave until just cool enough to handle. Peel off the skins with your fingers.

3 Make the anchovy dressing. In a large bowl, whisk together the oil, lemon juice and anchovy essence until thick. Stir in the onion, garlic, capers and anchovy fillets, if using.

4 Pour the dressing over the potatoes whilst they are still warm. Toss well and leave for about 30 minutes until completely cold. Taste and adjust seasoning before serving. Garnish with anchovy fillets.

Menu Suggestion
With its tangy dressing, this potato salad goes well with salami and rich cold meats such as pork.

INSALATA DI PATATE

The anchovy essence specified in this recipe is available in bottles or tubes at large supermarkets and delicatessens specialising in continental foods. It keeps indefinitely and is a useful store-cupboard ingredient in that it can be used to 'pep up' all kinds of dishes. It is especially good with the rather bland flavours of potatoes and eggs, and is excellent stirred into mayonnaise to give extra zing. Try a teaspoon or two in meat pâtés and loaves, or in home-made hamburgers.

Sweet Things

Desserts and pastries are
not usually eaten at the
end of everyday meals in
Italy—fresh fruit and
cheese are generally more
popular. The Italian
sweet tooth is well
catered for at other times
of day—with mid-
morning or afternoon
cups of espresso or
capuccino. For special
occasions, desserts are
often quite elaborate, but
it is the trend for cakes
and pastries to be bought
at the local patisserie, and
ice creams and bombes
from the *gelateria*. The
recipes in this chapter
will inspire you to make
your own *dolci*, a far more
rewarding experience
than buying them
ready-made.

PESCHE RIPIENE
(STUFFED PEACHES)

| 0.40 | 224 cals |

Serves 4

4 yellow peaches, skinned

50 g (2 oz) Amaretti (see box) or macaroons

1 egg yolk

25 g (1 oz) butter

25 g (1 oz) sugar

150 ml ($\frac{1}{4}$ pint) dry white wine

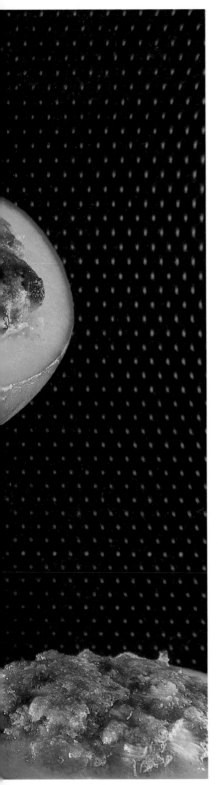

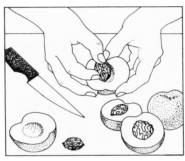

1 Cut the peaches in half and carefully ease out the stones with finger and thumb.

2 Make the hollows in the peaches a little deeper with a sharp-edged teaspoon and reserve the removed flesh.

3 Crush the macaroons and mix them with the reserved peach flesh, the egg yolk, butter and 15 g ($\frac{1}{2}$ oz) sugar.

4 Use this mixture to stuff the hollows of the peach halves, mounding the filling slightly.

5 Place the peaches in a lightly buttered ovenproof dish, and sprinkle with the rest of the sugar. Pour the white wine over and around the peaches.

6 Bake the peaches in the oven at 180° (350°F) mark 4 for 25–30 minutes or until tender. Serve hot or cold.

Menu Suggestion
Serve this fruity dessert after a rich main course such as Osso Buco (page 83).

PESCHE RIPIENE
Amaretti are almond macaroons made in Italy. They are available at Italian delicatessens, both in boxes and individually wrapped in tissue paper. They are delicious served with coffee and liqueurs at the end of a meal — the Italians like to eat them with the almond liqueur Amaretto (see page 143) — and can also be used in many sweet dishes and desserts such as this one.

ZUCCOTTO
(FLORENTINE TIPSY CAKE)

| 0.45* | £ £ | ✳ | 902 cals |

* plus 12 hours chilling

Serves 6

50 g (2 oz) blanched almonds

50 g (2 oz) hazelnuts

45 ml (3 tbsp) brandy

30 ml (2 tbsp) orange-flavoured
  liqueur

30 ml (2 tbsp) cherry- or almond-
  flavoured liqueur

350 g (12 oz) trifle sponges or
  Madeira cake

150 g (5 oz) plain chocolate

450 ml (15 fl oz) double cream

150 g (5 oz) icing sugar

25 g (1 oz) cocoa powder, to
  decorate

1 Spread the almonds and
 hazelnuts out separately on a
baking tray and toast in the oven
at 200°C (400°F) mark 6 for 5
minutes until golden.

2 Transfer the hazelnuts to a
 clean tea towel and rub off the
skins while still warm. Spread all
the nuts out to cool for 5 minutes
and then roughly chop.

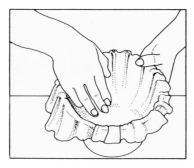

3 Line a 1.4-litre (2½-pint)
 pudding basin or round-
bottomed bowl with damp muslin.

4 In a separate bowl, mix
 together the brandy and the
liqueurs and set aside.

5 Split the trifle sponges in half
 through the middle (if using
Madeira cake, cut into 1 cm (½
inch) slices). Sprinkle with the
brandy and liqueurs.

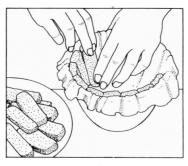

6 Line the basin with the
 moistened split sponges, reserving enough to cover the top.

7 Using a sharp knife, chop 75 g
 (3 oz) of the plain chocolate
into small pieces, and set aside.

8 In a separate bowl, whip the
 cream with 125 g (4 oz) icing
sugar until stiff and fold in the
chopped chocolate and nuts.

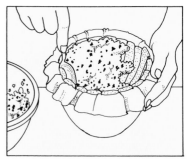

9 Divide this mixture in two and
 use one half to spread over the
sponge lining in an even layer.

10 Melt the remaining
 chocolate, cool slightly,
then fold into the remaining cream
mixture. Use this to fill the centre
of the pudding.

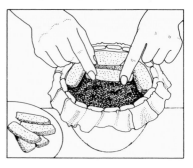

11 Level the top of the
 zuccotto and cover with the
remaining moistened sponge.
Trim edges. Cover and refrigerate for at least 12 hours.

12 To serve. Uncover, invert a
 flat serving plate over basin
and turn upside down. Lift off the
bowl, and carefully remove the
muslin. Serve cold, dusted with
the remaining icing sugar and
cocoa powder.

Menu Suggestion
A rich, creamy dessert to serve for
a special occasion meal after a light
main course such as Abbachio alla
Romana (page 88).

SALAME AL CIOCCOLATO
(CHOCOLATE 'SALAMI')

| 1.00* | 🝙 | £ £ | ✳* | 472–629 cals |

* plus 1 hour firming up and about 4 hours freezing; freeze at the end of step 6

Serves 6–8

50 g (2 oz) split blanched almonds

20 Petit Beurre biscuits

225 g (8 oz) plain chocolate, broken into small pieces

175 g (6 oz) unsalted butter, cut into small pieces

45 ml (3 tbsp) almond-flavoured liqueur (see page 143) or brandy

1 egg yolk

25 g (1 oz) ground almonds

1 Spread the blanched almonds out evenly in a grill pan and toast under a moderate grill for a few minutes until evenly browned. Shake the pan frequently so that the almonds do not burn.

2 Transfer the nuts to a nut grinder or food processor and work until finely ground.

3 Put the biscuits in a heavy bowl and crush roughly with the end of a rolling pin. Take out a handful of the crushed biscuits and set aside.

4 Put the chocolate pieces, butter and liqueur in a large heatproof bowl standing over a pan of gently simmering water. Heat gently until melted, stirring occasionally to combine the ingredients.

5 Pour the melted chocolate mixture into the bowl of crushed biscuits. Add the toasted nuts and egg yolk and mix well to combine. Leave in a cool place for about 1 hour to firm up.

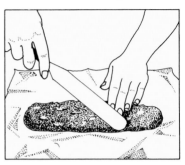

6 Turn the mixture out on to a large sheet of lightly buttered foil. With a palette knife and your hands, shape into a sausage about 23 cm (9 inches) long, with tapering ends. Wrap in the foil and freeze for about 4 hours or until the mixture is solid.

7 Crush the reserved biscuits very finely to a powder in an electric blender or food processor, then mix with the ground almonds.

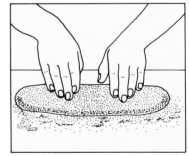

8 Unwrap the 'salami' and roll in the powder until evenly coated. Leave to stand for 1 hour before serving.

Menu Suggestion
A very rich chocolate confection, to be served at the end of a dinner party with coffee and liqueurs.

BUDINO DI RICOTTA ALLA ROMANA
(RICOTTA CHEESECAKE, ROMAN STYLE)

| 1.00* | £ £ | ✳* | 452 cals |

* plus 2–3 hours cooling; freeze after step 5

Serves 4

350 g (12 oz) **Ricotta or curd cheese**

3 **egg yolks, beaten**

100 g (4 oz) **sugar**

50 ml (2 fl oz) **rum or brandy**

50 g (2 oz) **ground almonds**

40 g (1½ oz) **chopped candied peel**

grated rind of 1 lemon

vanilla sugar, to decorate (see page 139)

1 Grease and flour a 20.5-cm (8-inch) cake tin and set aside until required.

2 Push the Ricotta or curd cheese through a sieve into a bowl, beat in the egg yolks and sugar.

3 Add the rum, beat well, then fold in the ground almonds, candied peel and lemon rind.

4 Pour into the prepared tin and bake in the oven at 180°C (350°F) mark 4 for 30–40 minutes or until firm and slightly shrunken from the sides of the tin.

5 Open the door of the oven and switch off. Leave the cheese-cake inside the oven for about 2–3 hours to cool with the door ajar.

6 To serve. Carefully remove the cheesecake from the tin and dredge with vanilla sugar.

Menu Suggestion

A rich cheesecake, the perfect finale to a special dinner party meal. Serve after a light main course such as Triglie al Cartoccio (page 77).

CENCI
(DEEP-FRIED PASTRY TWISTS)

0.45	🍴	£	43 cals

Makes 50

300 g (11 oz) plain flour

2 eggs, beaten

45 ml (3 tbsp) rum

60 ml (4 tbsp) caster sugar

5 ml (1 tsp) baking powder

pinch of salt

vegetable oil, for deep frying

icing or caster sugar, for sprinkling

1 Make the dough. Sift 250 g (9 oz) of the flour into a bowl. Make a well in the centre and add the next five ingredients.

2 Mix the ingredients well together with a fork until they come together as a dough.

3 Sprinkle the work surface with some of the remaining flour. Turn the dough out on to the floured surface and gather into a ball with your fingers. Knead until smooth.

4 Cut the dough into quarters. Roll out one quarter of the dough until almost paper thin, adding more flour to the work surface as necessary.

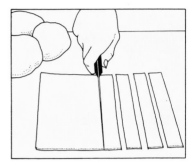

5 Cut into strips about 15 cm (6 inches) long and 2.5 cm (1 inch) wide.

6 Tie the strips into loose knots. Repeat rolling, cutting and tying with the remaining three quarters of dough.

7 Heat the oil in a deep-fat frier to 190°C (375°F). Add 4–5 of the pastry twists to the oil and deep-fry for 1–2 minutes until golden. Drain on absorbent paper while frying the remainder. Sift icing sugar over the twists while they are hot. Serve warm or cold.

Menu Suggestion
The Italians eat Cenci at any time of day, whenever they feel like a snack or something sweet to nibble. Children love them, and they are traditional at birthday parties and other celebrations.

ZUPPA INGLESE
(MARSALA AND CREAM TRIFLE)

1.45*	£ £	414–552 cals

* plus at least 4 hours chilling

Serves 6–8

568 ml (1 pint) milk
1 vanilla pod
4 eggs
50 g (2 oz) caster sugar
225 ml (8 fl oz) Marsala
150 ml (¼ pint) water
16 trifle sponge cakes
300 ml (10 fl oz) double cream
glacé cherries and angelica, to decorate

1 Make the custard. Scald the milk with the vanilla pod and immediately remove from the heat. Leave to infuse for 20 minutes, then strain.

2 Put the eggs and sugar in a heatproof bowl and lightly whisk together. Slowly pour in the milk, whisking all the time.

3 Stand the bowl over a pan of gently simmering water and stir until thick enough to coat the back of a spoon. (Be patient — this can take as long as twenty minutes.)

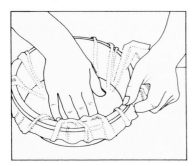

4 Remove the bowl from the heat, cover the surface of the custard closely with cling film and leave until cold.

5 Mix the Marsala and water together in a shallow dish. Dip a few of the trifle sponges in the liquid, then use them to line the bottom of a glass serving bowl.

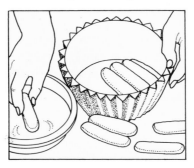

6 Pour one-third of the cold custard over the sponges. Dip a few more trifle sponges in the liquid and place on top of the custard. Cover with another third of the custard.

7 In a separate bowl, whip the cream until thick, then spread half over the custard.

8 Finish with a layer each of the remaining sponges and liquid, the custard and cream. Chill in the refrigerator for at least 4 hours, preferably overnight. Decorate with glacé cherries and angelica just before serving.

Menu Suggestion
Serve this boozy trifle for a dinner party dessert or special teatime treat — as you would any other trifle.

TORTA DI MELE
(GENOESE APPLE CAKE)

| 1.30* | ⬚ | ✳* | 456 cals |

* plus 2–3 hours cooling time; freeze after cooling in step 9

Serves 6

4 eggs

150 g (5 oz) caster sugar

150 g (5 oz) plain flour

5 ml (1 tsp) baking powder

pinch of salt

100 g (4 oz) butter, melted and cooled

90 ml (6 tbsp) milk

finely grated rind of 1 lemon

700 g (1½ lb) Golden Delicious apples, peeled, cored and thinly sliced

5–10 ml (1–2 tbsp) vegetable oil

15–30 ml (1–2 tbsp) dried breadcrumbs

icing sugar, to finish

1 Put the eggs and sugar in a heatproof bowl standing over a pan of gently simmering water.

2 Whisk for 10–15 minutes until the mixture is thick and pale and holds a ribbon trail when the beaters are lifted. (Alternatively, if you have a table top electric mixer, this can be used instead of whisking over hot water.)

3 Remove the bowl from the heat and continue whisking until the mixture is cool.

4 Sift the flour with the baking powder and salt. Fold half of this mixture gently into the whisked eggs and sugar.

5 Slowly trickle the melted butter around the edge of the bowl and fold it in gently. Take care not to stir too heavily or the mixture will lose air.

6 Fold in the remaining flour mixture, then the milk and lemon rind. Fold in the apples.

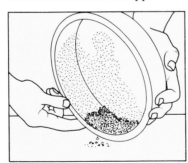

7 Brush the inside of a 23-cm (9-inch) diameter cake tin with oil. Sprinkle with breadcrumbs, then shake off the excess.

8 Pour the cake mixture into the tin and bake in the oven at 180°C (350°F) mark 4 for about 40 minutes until a skewer inserted in the centre comes out clean.

9 Leave the cake to rest in the tin for about 5 minutes, then turn out on to a wire rack and leave for 2–3 hours to cool completely. Sift icing sugar over the top of the cake just before serving.

Menu Suggestion
Serve plain with morning coffee or afternoon tea, or with fresh pouring cream as a dessert.

TORTA DI MELE
This recipe for a Genoese sponge, which is heavy with sweet dessert apples, is made in the classic way by whisking together eggs and sugar over heat until thick and mousse-like, then folding in sifted flour and finally trickling in melted butter. This method gives a light, airy result typical of any whisked or Genoese sponge. If you are in a hurry, you can cut corners with this particular recipe, because the weight of the apples tends to disguise the texture of the cake! Simply beat the eggs and sugar together with a wooden spoon, then fold in the flour mixture, followed by the melted butter, milk, lemon rind and apples.

GRANITA ALL' ARANCIA
(ORANGE WATER ICE)

| 0.25* | £ | ✳ | 161 cals |

* plus 8 hours freezing
Serves 6
175 g (6 oz) sugar
450 ml ($\frac{3}{4}$ pint) water
10 large oranges
1$\frac{1}{2}$ lemons

1 Make the sugar syrup. Place the sugar and water in a medium saucepan. Heat gently until the sugar dissolves, then boil gently for 10 minutes without stirring.

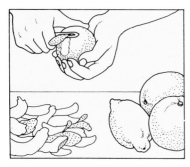

2 Meanwhile, using a potato peeler, thinly pare off the rind from four of the oranges and the lemons.

3 Add the orange and lemon rind to the sugar syrup and leave to go quite cold.

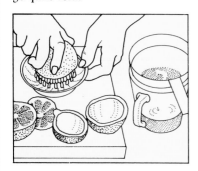

4 Squeeze the juice from the four oranges and the lemons. Strain into a measuring jug — there should be 450 ml ($\frac{3}{4}$ pint).

5 Strain the cold syrup into a shallow freezer container and stir in the fruit juices. Mix well, cover and freeze for about 4 hours until mushy in texture.

6 Remove from the freezer and turn the frozen mixture into a bowl. Beat well with a fork to break down the ice crystals. Return to the freezer container and freeze for at least 4 hours until the mixture is firm.

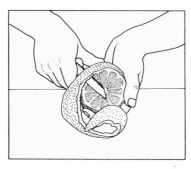

7 Meanwhile, using a serrated knife, cut away the peel and pith from the remaining oranges.

8 Slice the oranges down into thin rings, ease out and discard any pips. Place the oranges in a serving bowl; cover tightly with cling film and refrigerate until serving time.

9 Place the water ice in the refrigerator for 45 minutes to soften before serving. Serve with the fresh orange slices.

Menu Suggestion
Serve this tangy water ice for a dinner party dessert after a rich or substantial main course.

VARIATIONS

Granita al Limone
(Lemon Water Ice)
With 6–8 lemons as a basis, follow the recipe using the pared rind of four lemons and enough juice to give 450 ml ($\frac{3}{4}$ pint).

Granita di Fragole
(Strawberry Water Ice)
With 700 g (1$\frac{1}{2}$ lb) strawberries, puréed and sieved, and the pared rind and juice of 1 orange as a basis, follow the recipe, using the strawberry purée and orange juice instead of the orange and lemon juices in step 4.

Granita di Caffè
(Coffee Water Ice)
Put 30 ml (2 tbsp) sugar and 50 g (2 oz) finely ground Italian coffee in a jug, pour over 600 ml (1 pint) boiling water and leave to stand for 1 hour. Strain the coffee through a filter paper or muslin, then follow the recipe after the straining in step 5.

CASSATA
(ICE CREAM AND FRUIT BOMBE)

2.00* ☐ £ £ ✳ 332 cals

* plus 18–21 hours freezing, 2 hours macerating and 1 hour 30 minutes– 1 hour 40 minutes to soften

Serves 8

3 egg yolks

75 g (3 oz) caster sugar

300 ml (½ pint) milk, plus 15 ml (1 tbsp)

50 g (2 oz) plain chocolate

225 g (8 oz) ripe strawberries, sliced

1.25 ml (¼ tsp) vanilla flavouring

300 ml (10 fl oz) double cream

red food colouring

15 g (½ oz) pistachio nuts

4 glacé cherries

30 ml (2 tbsp) chopped mixed peel

30 ml (2 tbsp) orange-flavoured liqueur

1 Using a wooden spoon or rotary whisk, beat the egg yolks and caster sugar together until thick and pale in colour.

2 Make the custard. In a medium saucepan, scald 300 ml (½ pint) milk. Pour on to the egg mixture, stirring well. Return to the pan and cook over a low heat, *without boiling*, until the custard thickens slightly. Strain into a bowl and cool for 30 minutes.

3 Break up the chocolate and place with 15 ml (1 tbsp) milk in a bowl standing in a pan of hot water. Leave until chocolate melts. Add two-thirds of the cool custard to the chocolate, stirring to blend.

4 Purée the strawberries in a blender or food processor; sieve into the remaining custard and stir in the vanilla flavouring.

5 In a separate bowl, lightly whip 150 ml (5 fl oz) of the cream. Stir two-thirds of this through the cold chocolate mixture and the remainder into the strawberry, adding red colouring to the latter if necessary.

6 Pour the mixtures into separate shallow polythene containers and freeze for about 4 hours until mushy in texture.

7 When the mixtures are mushy, take them out of the freezer and turn them into separate bowls.

8 Beat vigorously with a whisk or wooden spoon to break down the ice crystals. Spoon back into the plastic containers, cover and freeze for a further 4–6 hours until quite firm.

9 Put a disc of non-stick paper in the base of a 1.1-litre (2-pint) pudding basin. Put empty basin into freezer. Leave chocolate ice cream at room temperature for about 20 minutes to soften slightly.

10 Line the basin evenly with chocolate ice cream, using a round-bowled spoon. Freeze for about 1 hour until firm.

11 Take the strawberry ice cream out of the freezer and leave at room temperature for 20–30 minutes to soften slightly.

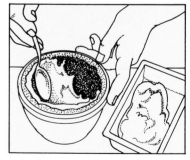

12 Work the strawberry ice cream with a spoon to make it more pliable (it will be firmer than the chocolate ice cream), then use to make a second lining of ice cream in the basin. Freeze, covered, for 1–2 hours until firm.

13 Pour boiling water over the pistachio nuts, leave to stand for 10 minutes, skin and chop roughly. Cut cherries into small pieces and macerate with the nuts, peel and liqueur for 2 hours, covered.

14 In a separate bowl, stiffly whisk the remaining cream and fold in the cherry mixture. Spoon into the centre of the cassata. Freeze, covered, for 4 hours.

15 Stand the pudding basin in a bowl of hot water for a few seconds to loosen the cassata. Slip a knife around the top edge to ensure it is loose and invert on to a serving platter; remove the paper. Leave in the refrigerator for about 40 minutes to 'come to'. Serve the cassata in wedges.

Menu Suggestion
A rich fruit and ice cream bombe for a special occasion dessert. Serve only after a plain or light main course dish.

CASSATA

Recipes for Cassata are confusing, because there are two different types. The recipe given here is for Cassata Gelata, which is an ice cream bombe. The other type is known as Cassata Siciliana and is a chilled dessert made from layers of Ricotta cheese and sponge cake. It is a Sicilian speciality which is traditionally served at Easter and other festivities such as weddings.

ZABAGLIONE
(MARSALA AND EGG DESSERT)

0.15	169 cals

Serves 6

4 egg yolks

65 g (2½ oz) caster sugar

100 ml (4 fl oz) Marsala

sponge fingers, to serve

1 Put the egg yolks and sugar in a large heatproof bowl. Beat together, then add the Marsala and beat until mixed.

2 Place the bowl over a saucepan of simmering water and heat gently, whisking the mixture until it is very thick and creamy.

3 To serve. Pour the zabaglione into six glasses and serve immediately, with sponge fingers.

Menu Suggestion
A classic, rich dessert to serve for a dinner party after a light main course such as grilled meat, poultry or fish.

USEFUL INFORMATION
AND
BASIC RECIPES

Specialist Ingredients

Cooking Italian-style is not difficult, and nowadays you will find it very easy to buy all the ingredients you need to make up the recipes in this book—Italian specialist shops, delicatessens, high-quality greengrocers and even supermarkets stock a wide range of Italian products, so with any luck you will have to look no further than your local high street.

The following chapter provides useful information to help you choose the correct ingredients when shopping, plus how to prepare them. It also offers ideas for substitutes and alternatives if for any reason you are unable to buy exactly what you need.

PASTA

The exact origins of pasta are uncertain. Some say that Marco Polo brought it to Europe from China, but this seems unlikely when we know there are historical records of the ancient Romans eating it in the fifth century BC! There are said to be over 500 different varieties throughout Italy, today, although only about 50 of these are widely known. The best commercially dried pasta is made from 100 per cent hard durum wheat *(semola di grano duro)*, so check this before buying.

As for nutritional value, pasta is of course mainly a carbohydrate food, although good-quality brands can contain as much as 13 per cent protein, and all contain some vitamins and minerals (a basic meal of spaghetti with tomato sauce, for example, is said to contain significant amounts of vitamin E—good for the skin as well as the reproductive organs!).

Ingredients vary from one brand to another, but in general the southern Italian varieties tend to be the tubular types which are not made with eggs, whereas the ones from the north of Italy are flat and usually made with the addition of eggs.

DIFFERENT TYPES OF PASTA

There is an increasingly wide choice of both fresh and dried pasta, now both in high street supermarkets as well as specialist pasta shops and Italian delicatessens. Although none of these quite compare with the flavour and freshness of homemade pasta (see recipe and cooking instructions on page 150), they are still mostly made with top-quality ingredients. Coloured pasta adds interest to meals—green pasta *(pasta verde)* is flavoured with spinach, and pink or red pasta *(pasta rosso)* with tomatoes. Wholemeal pasta is also available, which of course contains more fibre than pasta made with ordinary plain white flour, and is consequently more chewy and tasty. Choose according to personal taste and the kind of sauce you are serving it with.

The following list gives the most common pasta shapes, although you may see slightly different shapes or the same shape under different names—especially if you are actually visiting Italy itself. This is simply because the different regions of Italy have their own individual pasta shapes and names—and so do the different manufacturers.

PASTA LUNGA
(LONG PASTA)
The following long pasta are best served with smooth or fairly thick sauces. If the sauce is too thin it will slide off the pasta; if it has large chunks of fish or meat, their weight will cause the same thing to happen. Long pasta is therefore best served with a 'clinging'-type sauce such as a sauce made with melted butter and chopped herbs, or a smooth tomato, cream- or milk-based sauce. If you want to add other ingredients such as ham or shellfish, cut them finely.

Capelli d'angelo: one of the finest of the long pastas, hence the name of angel's hair. Often sold coiled into nests *(a nidi)* or under the name **capellini**.

Lasagne: the broadest of the flat noodles, which comes plain, ridged and with crinkled edges. Spinach-flavoured *(lasagne verdi)* is common. Lasagne is the one kind of long pasta which is never served with a sauce at the table, but always baked in the oven *(al forno)* in layers with a sauce. Always check packets of dried lasagne—some are pre-cooked and can be baked without pre-boiling.

Maccheroni: a thicker, hollow version of spaghetti. Sold long in Italy, but exported macaroni is mostly in cut or short form.

Spaghetti: thin strings of pasta (from the Italian word for string, *spago*), without holes. Comes in different thicknesses according to region of manufacture. Thin spaghetti from southern Italy is known as **vermicelli**.

Tagliatelle: flat ribbon noodles from northern Italy. Available with egg *(all'uovo)* or spinach *(verdi)* and often coiled into nests *(a nidi)*. **Fettuccine** is the Roman version of tagliatelle. **Paglia e fieno** are nests of white and green tagliatelle or fettuccine packed together.

PASTA CORTA
(SHORT/CUT PASTA AND PASTA SHAPES)
These are easier to serve (and eat!) than the long varieties, so your choice of sauce is not quite so crucial. Cut pasta and pasta shapes are ideal for heavy sauces which contain large chunks of meat and fish, and are perfect for baked and composite dishes.

Cannelloni: large hollow tubes for stuffing and baking in a sauce. Lasagne can be used in recipes calling for cannelloni—simply spread the stuffing on the flat noodle, then roll it up.

Conchiglie: pasta in the shape of seashells which are excellent for trapping chunky sauces. In many different sizes.

Farfalle: in the shape of a bow-tie, often with a crinkled edge. **Farfallette** are a diminutive version.

Fusilli: spiral-shaped pasta which come in many different shapes and sizes, some of which look like coils. **Spirale ricciolo** are similar.

Maccheroni: known as 'elbow' macaroni, it comes in many different lengths and thicknesses, some of which are quick-cooking.

Penne: hollow pasta shaped like quills with angled ends. Available ridged and plain.

Cappelletti: the word means 'little hats'. Stuffings vary from chicken or pork to mortadella sausage and cheese.

Ravioli: small, square or round shapes, often with crinkled edges. Stuffing is usually meat, or spinach and Ricotta cheese.

Tortellini: also called **tortelli** and **tortelloni**, look like twisted rings or navels. Stuffings are the same as for cappelletti.

PASTINA *(SOUP PASTA)*
Very tiny shapes which are used only in soups. Shapes vary from bow-ties (**farfallette**) and wheels (**rotellini**) to the tiny rings (**anellini**) and stars (**stellette**).

Rigatoni: tubular, like short maccheroni with ridges. Comes in different thicknesses.

Rotelle: wheel-shaped pasta, most popular outside Italy.

PASTA RIPIENA *(STUFFED PASTA)*
Experiment with different brands to find the ones you like the best. Stuffed pasta is excellent for quick or impromptu meals because all it needs is melted butter and a sprinkling of herbs and Parmesan cheese, or a light sauce.

PASTA SHAPES

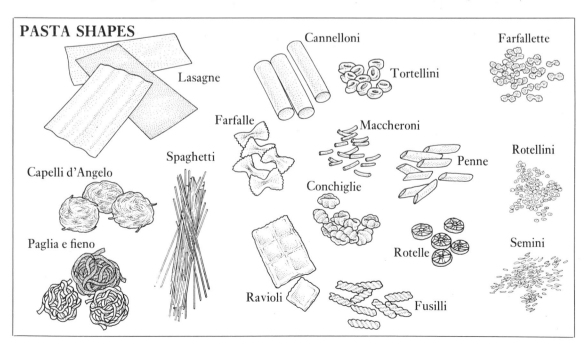

Lasagne · Cannelloni · Tortellini · Farfallette · Capelli d'Angelo · Spaghetti · Farfalle · Maccheroni · Penne · Rotellini · Conchiglie · Paglia e fieno · Rotelle · Semini · Ravioli · Fusilli

RICE

Italian rice is quite unique, and so too is the Italian method of cooking it in the form of risotto. The Italians like to cook risotto with plenty of liquid, adding it a little at a time and stirring it constantly so that the end result is creamy and almost sticky—called *all'onda* in Italian. To achieve this consistency a special kind of short grain rice is necessary, which swells during cooking with the gradual addition of liquid, and which does not break up through constant stirring. The grains of rice must cling together for a perfect risotto, which is the reverse of most savoury rice dishes, in which long grain rice should be fluffy and the grains separate.

The best kind of rice to use for risotto is called **arborio**, which comes from the rice fields of the

Italian 'risotto' rice

Po valley in Piedmont, northern Italy. This region is the biggest rice-producing area in Italy, and the northern Italians are consequently the biggest rice-eaters (the southerners prefer pasta!). Look for arborio in specialist delicatessens and Italian shops, where you may also find two other varieties called **superfino** and **avorio**—these are pre-fluffed and a golden yellow colour rather like easy-cook long grain rice, the perfect varieties of rice to buy if you are unaccustomed to risotto making. Boxes of rice labelled 'Italian risotto rice' are also available at supermarkets; they usually contain arborio rice, or a rice of

similar quality. Italians also use this type of rice for stuffings and Timballo (see recipe on page 64).

As well as risotto, Italians also eat plain boiled rice in the way that we do, but in Italy this is never eaten with a main course as a vegetable dish, but served as a first course, usually with a sauce poured over, or as a simple dish of Riso in Bianco—with melted butter and freshly grated Parmesan cheese. If you want to try this very simple dish to serve as a starter (it's really delicious before an Italian main course), buy rice labelled **fino** in your Italian shop and boil it in plenty of water, then drain it before serving as above.

POLENTA

Polenta is best described as a kind of yellow porridge made with cornmeal or maize flour, which is called *granturco* in Italian. Look for it in Italian shops, continental delicatessens and health food shops, often labelled simply 'polenta'. There are usually three varieties available—fine, medium and coarse. The coarser the polenta the brighter the colour. 'Instant' polenta is also available, which cooks in just 5 minutes, although polenta-lovers say it is no substitute for the real thing. Polenta is eaten all over northern Italy (but particularly in Piedmont and Lombardy, and in Venice where they use white maize flour rather than yellow). The southern Italians are not so fond of it, and even go so far as to jokingly nickname the northern Italians *polentoni*—the polenta-eaters!

Polenta is made simply by boiling the flour in salted water; it tastes rather bland, so is usually served as an accompaniment to strong-flavoured foods such as game birds, spicy sausage, cheese, or dishes which have lots of sauce.

The best way to cook polenta is in a special large pot called a **paiolo**. Polenta isn't difficult to make, but it does tend to splutter and spit while cooking, and the shape of the paiolo helps with this

problem. Paiolos are not generally sold outside Italy, but the best alternative is a large tall pan with a heavy base—a preserving pan is ideal. Polenta needs to be stirred constantly during cooking to prevent lumps forming, and a long-handled wooden spoon is therefore

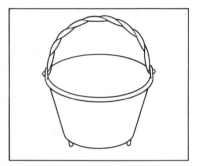

Paiolo

essential. Immediately the polenta is cooked, it is turned out and served on a special board called a **tafferia**, then cut into slices with a special wooden knife. A bread board and ordinary cook's knife can of course be used for this.

If you find plain boiled polenta rather uninspiring, the best way to

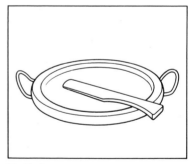

Tafferia

eat it is fried or grilled with a sauce or strong-flavoured cheese—the Italians love serving leftover polenta in this way. Turn back to the recipe for Polenta Fritta (page 71), which gives instructions for boiling polenta and frying it after it has gone cold, which you will find is absolutely delicious as a first course or snack.

CURED MEATS, SALAMI AND SAUSAGE

Preserved meats and salami feature prominently in the cuisine of Italy (particularly in the antipasto course) and each region has its own specialities. Fresh and preserved sausages are also immensely popular, particularly in the north. Many of these are exported and you will find a wide choice at Italian shops and delicatessens, and some large supermarkets. On this page are listed the most readily available types and the ones used in recipes in this book, plus some suggestions for substitutes if you find them hard to obtain.

Cotechino: a fresh sausage from Emilia-Romagna in northern Italy. A mixture of pork and spices, it goes particularly well with the bland flavour of potatoes and lentils, and is traditionally served with these in Italy. Some cotechino needs to be boiled for at least 3 hours, but look for **cotechino lampo**, which is precooked and only needs about 20 minutes boiling. Serve it sliced hot for a simple, but very tasty lunch or supper dish.

Luganega: a fresh sausage *(salsiccia)*, which is traditionally made in long lengths called **salsiccia a metro** (sausage by the metre) and is bought by the kg (lb). Link sausage, sometimes called **salamelle**, and made from the same mixture, is also sold. Both can be grilled or fried as any other fresh sausage. Most Italian *salsiccia* is spicy; some varieties are peppery hot—check before buying!

Mortadella: this familiar pale pink sausage with specks of fat, black peppercorns and sometimes pistachio nut, is one of Italy's most famous exports, and the largest of all the cured pork sausages. From Bologna in the north, where it is in fact called **bologna** rather than mortadella, the quality of this sausage varies enormously, from one manufacturer to another. The best mortadella or bologna is made from pure pork, although there are other kinds which contain beef, offal and cereals. Buy from an Italian specialist shop to be sure of getting good quality.

Pancetta: salted raw belly of pork, available only at Italian shops. It looks rather like streaky bacon and can be bought in long rasher form or rolled up. Slices of good-quality lean pancetta are often included in a meat antipasto,

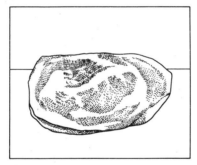

Pancetta

but most pancetta is chopped and used for frying in cooked dishes—its distinctive smoky flavour and aroma lend an authentic Italian touch to sauces, soups and stuffings, and it goes especially well with onions, garlic and tomatoes. Use pancetta sparingly, however, or its strong flavour will override the other ingredients in a dish. If you are unable to buy pancetta, use smoked streaky bacon instead. Another Italian pork product which is used for frying in cooked dishes is **lardo**, a pure pork back fat, only available in Italian shops. Remove the rind and chop the fat, then fry slowly until the fat runs. Discard any crisp pieces of fat before adding further ingredients.

Prosciutto: this is the Italian word for ham. Most of the prosciutto on sale in Italian shops is air-dried, which gives it a wonderful smoky flavour—boiled hams sold in supermarkets make poor substitutes and should not be used in a meat antipasto instead of prosciutto. **Prosciutto di Parma** is the most famous of all the hams—and the most expensive! Genuine Parma ham comes from the area around the twon of Parma in Emilia-Romagna, and must have its brand burned into the skin. All Parma hams have been dried for at least 8 months, some as long as 2 years, which gives them such a sweet, smoky flavour and tender flesh. Two similar types of ham are **prosciutto di San Daniele** and **coppa**, which are usually less expensive and some say equally delicious—perfect as part of an antipasto or served simply with melon or figs. If you see **Bresàola** in Italian shops, don't mistake this for prosciutto, it is in fact raw beef which has been cured and dried in much the same way. Although expensive, it makes the most delicious starter served simply sprinkled with olive oil, lemon juice and freshly ground black pepper.

Salami: the Italians are justifiably famous for their salami, which they most often eat as an antipasto before a meal. There are literally hundreds if not thousands of different shapes, sizes and flavours—some of the best are the coarse-textured homemade ones *(salame casalingo)*, which are only available in specialist Italian shops. From the fairly mild and finely minced to the coarse and spicy laced with pepper and garlic, names to look for when choosing salami to make up an antipasto are Genova, Napoli, Milano and Felino. **Pepperoni** is a pork and beef sausage, hot with red pepper; it is excellent in risottos and on pizza toppings.

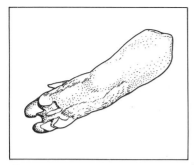

Zampone

Zampone: the same as cotechino (see page 133) except that it is stuffed into a pig's trotter rather than the usual type of sausage casing. Although a fairly fatty sausage, it is considered a great delicacy in Italy, and is well worth trying, especially the pre-cooked variety, **zampone lampo**, which does not need soaking and lengthy boiling.

CHEESES

Soft and creamy, sharp and blue, strong and crumbly—Italian cheeses are extremely varied in flavour and texture. Many of the best are local, fresh cheeses which are not exported, but there is an increasingly wide choice available, especially at Italian shops and delicatessens specialising in continental cheeses. Some large supermarkets stock the better known cheeses, but for choice and consistent quality, it is best to buy from the specialist. The following cheeses are the ones most commonly found outside Italy, and the ones used in the recipe section of this book.

Bel Paese: from the beautiful countryside of Lombardy in northern Italy (literally translated, *bel paese* means 'beautiful country'), this cow's milk cheese was invented in 1929, and is now made in factories and exported on a huge scale. Mild but fruity in flavour, with a soft creamy paste which is almost white in colour,

Bel Paese is excellent both as a table cheese and for cooking; it

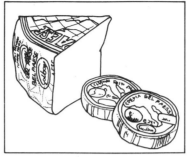

Bel Paese

also has exceptionally good keeping qualities. It has similar melting properties to Mozzarella and can be used as a substitute for it. Bel Paese is also a wise choice for a cheeseboard to serve as a contrast to a sharp, blue-veined cheese such as Gorgonzola.

Fontina: one of the most famous of all the Italian cheeses, from the Val d'Aosta region in north-west Italy. (The name Fontina comes from Mount Fontin near the town of Aosta). A semi-hard, ivory-coloured cow's milk cheese, Fontina has a deliciously nutty flavour, sweetish aroma and a smooth, creamy texture broken with a few 'eyes'. It can be used as a table cheese, but it is better known for its uses in cooking. It is the classic melting cheese to use in the Italian cheese 'dip' *fonduta*, just as Gruyère is in the Swiss fondue. Fontina has good keeping qualities; when mature and hard, it can be grated.

Gorgonzola: next to Parmesan, probably *the* most famous of the Italian cheeses. An alpine cheese made from cow's milk, Gorgonzola was originally made over a thousand years ago, when it was matured naturally in the damp caves around the village of Gorgonzola in Lombardy, a process which could take anything up to a year. Nowadays, Gorgonzola is made in factories in

and around the city of Milan and also in the region of Piedmont, where, with the help of the bacteria *Penicillium gorgonzola*, the maturing only takes three months. Today's factory-made cheese is creamy in texture, a blue-veined cheese with a mild tang which is not too salty. An excellent table cheese, it can also be melted and used in cooked dishes. Look for two kinds in specialist shops: **Gorgonzola piccante** (sharp) and **dolce** (sweet). **Dolcelatte** is a type of Gorgonzola, also factory made. Its name literally means 'sweet milk', which is an apt description of this popular mild, creamy cheese. **Stracchino** is yet another member of the large Gorgonzola family, although it is not generally a blue-veined cheese. From the Italian dialect word *stracco* meaning 'tired', this cheese is made from the milk of the 'tired' cows which come down from the Italian Alps to spend the winter grazing on the pastures around the city of Milan. A cheese which is gaining popularity is a layered cheese of Gorgonzola and creamy Mascarpone (see below). Look for it under the names **San Gaudenzio** or **Gorgonzola alla panna**, although it is often simply described as **Torta** because of its resemblance to a cake. This cheese makes an unusual addition to a cheeseboard.

Mascarpone: primarily a dessert cheese. Made from fresh cream, it originated in Lombardy, where it

Mascarpone

used to be made only during the autumn and winter, and was always sold in muslin bags. Nowadays it is exported in tubs, and is best described as a very thick, tasty cream—ideal for serving with fresh fruit and sugar. The Italians often mix Mascarpone with a liqueur such as Strega, and it is now available layered with such varied ingredients as Gorgonzola (see above), peppers, truffles, walnuts, herbs or garlic, in which case it is colloquially called **Torta di Formaggi** (cheese cake).

Mozzarella: was originally a buffalo milk cheese from the south, but cow's milk Mozzarella, or a mixture of both, is now more common. A fresh cheese which is sold in its own whey, in Italy Mozzarella comes in many different shapes and sizes, but outside Italy it is generally sold in the familiar waxed paper wrapping which is tied at the top. To eat fresh, Mozzarella should be no more than a day old; after this

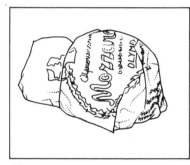

Mozzarella

time it becomes dry and is really only fit for cooking. Italian Mozzarella is now easy to obtain in supermarkets, but Bel Paese can be used as a substitute, so too can Danish or Scottish Mozzarella, which are widely available. None of these has quite the same 'stringy' melting qualities of Italian Mozzarella, however, so try to obtain the real thing if possible. **Smoked Mozzarella** and **Scamorza** make interesting additions to a cheeseboard.

Parmesan: possibly the most famous of Italian cheeses, and said to be the best of a group known collectively as *grana*—meaning hard and grainy. These cheeses

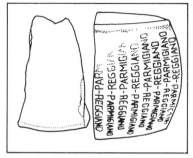

Parmesan

are produced only in Emilia-Romagna and Lombardy, and are primarily for grating and cooking, although very young cheeses can be used for the table. There are many different types of *grana* cheese, although **Grana Padano** (from the Po valley) is the one you are most likely to find outside Italy. Genuine Parmesan can only be made in and around the town of Parma, and it must bear the stamp *Parmigiano Reggiano* on its rind—check before buying. Parmesan is the most expensive of the *grana* cheeses, mainly because it takes the longest time to mature—at least 2 years. Always buy fresh Parmesan for grating; the types sold ready grated in drums and packets cannot compare for flavour with Parmesan cut fresh from a large piece. Look for cheese which is pale buff-yellow in colour, not too crumbly in texture.

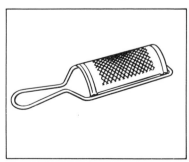

Parmesan grater

If you buy a large piece weighing, say, 450 g (1 lb), wrap it in a double thickness of foil or cling film and store it in the refrigerator—it will keep fresh for weeks. It can also be kept in the freezer for up to 3 months, in which case it is best to wrap it in smaller, more usable amounts. When you need grated Parmesan, simply cut off the required amount and grate it fresh with a special Parmesan grater, or the finest side of a conical or box grater (not a rotary grater). Never store the cheese grated or it will quickly lost its flavour and aroma.

Pecorino: a hard, grating and cooking cheese like Parmesan. A country ewe's milk cheese, it is believed to be one of the oldest of Italian cheeses—a recipe has been found for **Pecorino Romano** from as long ago as the first century AD! There are many different varieties of Pecorino, and Romano is considered to be the best; but look also for **Pecorino Sardo** (from Sardinia) which, along with **Pecorino pepato** (with peppercorns), is exported all over the world. A good Pecorino cheese has a compact, straw-yellow rind; avoid any that is very crumbly and dry looking, which means that it has been kept too long—most Pecorinos mature within 8 months.

Provolone: the most famous of the 'plastic-curd' cheese or *pasta filata* as they are known in Italian. These mildly flavoured table cheeses are made from pulling, kneading and moulding the curds of cow's milk, which have been made elastic by immersion in hot water and whey. The original Provolone cheese was oval in shape (the word provolone means 'large sphere'), but nowadays the most fanciful of shapes are made. Two of the best known are **Provola**, a smaller version of Provolone which looks rather like a pear or large egg, and **Caciocavallo**, which looks like two saddlebags. All cheeses in the

Caciocavallo

pasta filata family are tied with a cord, which leaves an impression in the cheese when it is removed. Although a table cheese, when mature and hard, Provolone can be grated and used in cooking.

Ricotta: not really a cheese at all, because it is traditionally made from the whey rather than the curd of milk, but nowadays whole or skimmed milk is added and it is sold and used as a cheese. Pure white in colour and bland in flavour, Ricotta is sometimes eaten as a fresh cheese in Italy with fresh fruit and sugar, but it is mostly used as a cooking cheese, particularly in the south where it is frequently mixed with other ingredients and used as a stuffing for pasta. It can be made of cow's, ewe's or goat's milk. Cottage cheese or curd cheese can be used as a substitute for Ricotta, and although these do not have the same slightly sweetish flavour, their texture is quite similar. **Ricotto al Forno** is an oven-baked table cheese which makes an interesting-looking addition to a cheeseboard.

Taleggio: a table cheese from Lombardy which is difficult to obtain in good condition outside Italy (it should be eaten young and and does not travel well). When just ripe, it has a wonderfully creamy paste and a subtle 'bite' to it. Worth looking for in specialist cheese shops.

VEGETABLES, PULSES AND FUNGHI

Artichokes, globe *(carciofi)*: an immensely popular vegetable in Italy, especially in the south where the Mediterranean climate suits it best. Small Italian artichokes are often a pretty purple in colour; young, tender and chokeless, these are delicious eaten whole, either fried simply in olive oil and seasoning, or served cold in a dressing as part of an antipasto course. Young, tender artichoke hearts are also served in this way. Larger artichokes are served stuffed (either hot or cold) for a first course, or sometimes sliced and fried as a vegetable dish.

Asparagus *(asparagi)*: young, tender asparagus spears can be seen in vegetable markets all over sunny Italy in early summer, and they require very little preparation other than a little gentle scraping at the base of their stems. Italians, especially the Venetians and the Milanese, love the combination of asparagus with eggs, and there are numerous ways to serve them as a starter—all simple dishes which allow the diner to appreciate the delicate flavour of the asparagus itself. One of the most popular is Asparagi alla Milanese—lightly cooked asparagus spears topped with fried eggs, melted butter and grated Parmesan cheese.

Aubergines *(melanzane)*: come in a multitude of different shapes, sizes and colours in Italy. From plump and shiny, deep-purple ones, to long, thin white ones streaked with lilac, the choice is enormous, and it seems there are equally as many different ways to serve them. Stuffed aubergines (either hot or cold) are a favourite starter, so too are thin slices of aubergine fried in olive oil with garlic and breadcrumbs—served cold, these make a delicious

addition to an antipasto course. Italians love the combination of aubergines with tomatoes and cheese—particularly Parmesan and Mozzarella — and one of Italy's most famous vegetable recipes, Melanzane alla Parmigiana, combines these four ingredients in the same dish. Young aubergines need no preparation before cooking, but older specimens need to be *dégorgéed* to help remove any bitter juices they may contain. Slice them thinly, then place them in a colander, sprinkling each layer with salt. Put a plate on top, weight it down, then leave to drain for 30 minutes. Rinse and dry before use.

Chicory, red *(radicchio)*: although white and pale green chicory is grown, it is the red chicory—radicchio—which is unique to Italy. There are many different varieties, not all of which are available outside Italy, but which are well worth looking for in specialist markets and greengrocers—or you can grow them yourself from seed in the garden. You may find a red version of the torpedo-shaped Belgian chicory, but the prettiest kinds of radicchio are **rossa di Treviso**, tulip-shaped and streaked red and cream, and **rossa di Verona**, which is rounder and deeper red or even maroon in colour. Radicchio looks beautiful crisp and raw in salads, especially when contrasted with a green leafy vegetable such as lettuce or curly endive. The Italians also serve radicchio braised as a hot vegetable dish, but this way it loses its attractive colour. Always use it sparingly—it is even more bitter than white chicory.

Courgettes *(zucchini)*: a popular vegetable for stuffing in Italy; in fact they grow so profusely, that even the flower heads are stuffed! Cheese, breadcrumbs, meat (including chicken livers) and herbs are common stuffings, and they can be served hot or cold, either as a starter or as a vegetable dish. Young, tender courgettes are sliced thinly and fried in olive oil and garlic—sprinkled with breadcrumbs and served cold, they also make a tasty addition to an Antipasto Misto. Never peel courgettes before cooking or you will throw away most of their flavour!

Fennel *(finocchio)*: originally from the city of Florence, this is correctly described as 'Florence fennel' to distinguish it from the feathery herb of the same name. The Florentines like to serve this delicate, aniseed-tasting bulb very simply, gently boiled until tender yet still crisp, then sprinkled with melted butter and Parmesan. Other Italian ways of serving fennel are baked in the oven *(al forno)*, sometimes with a cheese or tomato sauce, and raw in salads.

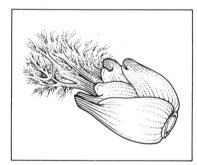

Florence fennel

To prepare fennel, simply slice off the feathery tops (reserve them for a garnish) and the root end, then leave whole, cut into halves or quarters lengthways, or slice into rounds and push out into rings.

Mushrooms, dried *(porcini)*: Italians love the strong 'earthy' flavour of dried mushrooms, especially in sauces, soups, stuffings and omelettes, and in pizza toppings. If a recipe specifies porcini then these must be used— fresh mushrooms will not have the required amount of flavour and aroma. Unlike other dried ingredients, porcini are not an inferior alternative—they are in fact an expensive, luxury item to be used sparingly. (Some Italian cooks

even add a few porcini to dishes which contain fresh mushrooms, just to give them more of a 'mushroomy' flavour.) Packets of porcini (wild *Boletus edulis* or cèpe in French) are available at all Italian shops and delicatessens; they

Soaking dried mushrooms

should be soaked in warm water for about 20 minutes before use. Only cook them for a short time or they lose their unique flavour.

Peppers *(peperoni)*: sweet red, green and yellow varieties grow profusely in the south of Italy, where the hot sun is just perfect for ripening. Not surprisingly, there are literally hundreds of different ways to cook and serve them, and Italians especially love them with other sun-ripened vegetables such as tomatoes, aubergines and courgettes. One of the tastiest ways to cook them is to grill them (preferably over charcoal) until the skins blister and burst, then skin the flesh and slice it into strips. After marinating in olive oil, lemon juice and garlic, they make a colourful antipasto. Stuffed peppers are also often

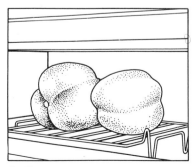

Grilling peppers

served as an antipasto, as is the famous dish of peppers and tomatoes—Peperonata (see recipe on page 98). **Peperoncini** (hot chilli peppers) are grown in southern Italy, and used in both fresh and dried form, especially in sauces for pasta and toppings for pizza. Always use them sparingly.

Pulses *(legumi secchi)*: used extensively in Italian cooking, but especially in thick, wintry soups. Fresh loose beans are used, and the canned varieties, which are popular, despite being more expensive, because they are quick and convenient to use—and tenderness is guaranteed every time. Italian shops, continental delicatessens and health food shops sell the best selection of the following pulses, although large supermarkets sell an increasingly wide range. **Borlotti beans** are speckled and pink or red in colour, from the same family as the red kidney bean. **Cannellini** beans are elongated in shape, white in colour, and one of the most popular pulses in Italy. French dried white haricot are similar and can be used as a substitute. **Garbanzos** are chickpeas—traditionally served with salt cod *(baccalà)* on Good Friday. **Fave secche** are dried broad beans; not easy to obtain outside continental countries, but worth looking for in Middle Eastern and oriental shops, as they are good in puréed soups. **Lenticchie** are the green 'continental' lentils as opposed to the red or split varieties. Italians eat them with Bollito Misto (a dish of mixed meats), and with sausages such as zampone and cotechino.

Tomatoes *(pomodori)*: these dominate the cuisine of Italy, especially in the sunny south. Fresh and canned, in paste or purée form, tomatoes are used as an essential flavouring in countless savoury dishes. In summertime the large juicy, misshapen varieties are used fresh, mostly in salads. Their flavour is unbelievably sweet, and the combination of fresh tomatoes and basil is an all-time favourite with the Italians— as is the combination of tomatoes and Mozzarella cheese. Look for

'Plum' and 'beefsteak' tomatoes

these tomatoes, labelled 'continental' or 'beefsteak', in specialist markets and greengrocers. For cooking, Italians grow 'plum' tomatoes. Soft, juicy and full of flavour they are incomparable, especially in sauces. Outside Italy, we usually have to make do with canned ones, as the fresh ones do not travel well enough for them to be exported on a large scale.

Truffles *(tartufi)*: as expensive in Italy as anywhere else, and just as highly prized. Truffles from the region of Piedmont are considered to be one of the best varieties in the world. These are the white ones, most of which are found in the forest around Alba. (The French prefer the black variety from Périgord.) White truffles are more highly perfumed than the black, in fact both their aroma and flavour are quite powerful in comparison. For this reason they are always used in very small quantities, usually grated on to pasta dishes, omelettes and risottos, or served sparingly with chicken, veal and beef dishes.

HERBS, SPICES AND FLAVOURINGS

There are a number of herbs, spices and other flavourings which are used over and over again in Italian cookery; to give your Italian dishes an 'authentic' flavour, these are essential. Most of them will be in your store cupboard already, so it is unlikely that you will have to buy many more.

HERBS
Different herbs are used in the different regions of Italy, and are often connected with specific dishes. Fresh herbs are more widely used than dried, especially in the south where they grow so profusely in the sunny, mild climate.

Basil *(basilico)*: one of Italy's most favourite herbs, it is used extensively in cooking. Tomatoes have a special affinity with basil, and almost all tomato soups and sauces are flavoured with this

Basil

herb. One of Italy's most famous sauces—Pesto—from Liguria, is made with large quantities of basil. For the sweetest flavour, use fresh basil—an annual plant which will grow happily in a pot on a sunny windowsill in the kitchen. Dried sweet basil can also be used, but only buy in small quantities as it quickly goes stale.

Bay *(alloro/lauro)*: fresh and dried bay leaves are used sparingly to flavour sauces, casseroles and soups, and are always discarded before serving. Bay trees are worth having in the garden—shiny fresh bay leaves make an attractive garnish as well as a flavouring.

Borage *(boraggine)*: only used fresh, borage is eaten like spinach. With a flavour similar to cucumber, in Italy it is often included in stuffings for pasta such as ravioli, and is also popular fried in batter. Borage is a useful herb to have in the garden for salads, and for floating on summer drinks and punches.

Chervil *(cerfoglio)*: similar in appearance to parsley, but with a more subtle flavour. The Italians like the flavour of chervil with cheese; it also mixes well with other herbs. Grow it annually from seed—dried chervil is virtually tasteless.

Fennel, wild *(finocchiella)*: the stems and leaves of this herb are used extensively, especially in sauces and stuffings. Fennel has a particular affinity with fish, eggs and mayonnaise. The seeds of fennel are a popular flavouring for pork, and are often found in Italian sausages and cooked meats. For information about the vegetable bulb fennel—finocchio —see page 137.

Marjoram, sweet *(maggiorana)*: the slightly spicy, sweet flavour of this herb is liked in fish dishes, but it is wild marjoram (oregano—see opposite) that is most often used.

Mint *(menta)* and **Peppermint** *(mentuccia)*: a favourite with the Romans and still used in Roman cooking. Can be used fresh with fish and vegetables, or in stuffings for pasta with cheese, also salads and soups. In Florence the local variety is called *nepitella*. All mints have a good flavour when they are dried.

Mixed herbs, dried *(erbe miste)*: a mixture of marjoram, parsley, sage, tarragon and thyme, dried mixed herbs should be used sparingly. The combination of dried mixed herbs and oregano is good in ragù (Bolognese sauce).

Oregano *(origano)*: the wild version of marjoram, a very aromatic herb, which is used as much as basil in Italian cooking, particularly in the south. Any dish containing tomatoes will benefit from the flavour of oregano, and it is very popular as a flavouring for pizzas and for sauces for pasta. Fresh oregano is rarely found outside Italy, but dried oregano has a good flavour and makes a perfectly acceptable substitute.

Parsley *(prezzemolo)*: the flat-leaved variety is grown in Italy, and it has a more pungent flavour

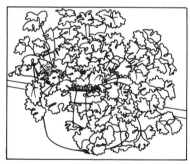

Parsley

than the curly or moss varieties. It is used in numerous savoury dishes, particularly in sauces and stuffings, combined with other herbs. Grow it from seed in the garden in summer, or look for it in greengrocers under the name 'continental' parsley.

Rosemary *(rosmarino)*: popular with grilled and roasted poultry, lamb and pork, but always used sparingly because of its highly pungent flavour. Particularly associated with Tuscany and all of central Italy. Buy a small bush from a nursery; it is an easy herb to grow in the garden.

Sage *(salvia)*: used in both fresh and dried forms, but never powdered. Most often used in the north with butter and cream sauces to serve with pasta; also popular with liver and veal.

Thyme *(timo)*: used all over Italy as a general flavouring for sauces, stuffings, etc. Both fresh and dried forms are used.

SPICES

Spices are not so widely used in Italian cooking as herbs, but nevertheless they do have their own place in the cuisine of the country. The following spices are the ones most frequently used.

Cinnamon *(cannelli)*: sometimes used ground in stuffed pasta dishes which have meat or cheese fillings. Cinnamon sticks are occasionally used for flavouring sweet dishes.

Juniper *(ginepro)*: the berries are crushed and used in marinades for pork and game, particularly in the north of Italy, where the juniper is said to be exceptionally strong in flavour.

Nutmeg *(noce moscata)*: probably the most commonly used spice, both in sweet and savoury dishes. Italians rarely use ready grated nutmeg, but prefer to grate whole nutmegs fresh every time on a special nutmeg grater. No Italian spinach or cheese dish seems complete without its sprinkling of freshly grated nutmeg.

Pepper *(pepe)*: Italians never use ready ground pepper. Whole peppercorns are always ground fresh every time in a pepper mill. Black peppercorns are most often used, the stronger-tasting white peppercorns are reserved for white or pale-coloured sauces. Ground red pepper *(pepe forte)* is extremely hot and should be used with caution; it is mostly found in southern Italian cooking, especially in sauces.

Saffron *(zafferano)*: from the stamens of the crocus. The most expensive spice in the world, and therefore used sparingly. Saffron is a classic ingredient of many risottos and fish stews, and ground turmeric should *never* be used as a substitute; saffron is delicate in flavour and colour, whereas turmeric is just the opposite. In Italy, two types of saffron are used: threads, which must be steeped in warm water for at least 30 minutes before use, and powder, which is added straight to a dish by the pinch. Sachets of powdered saffron are available from Italian delicatessens and are inexpensive and convenient to use, but are considered inferior to the saffron threads.

Salt *(sale)*. Not a spice, but a mineral. Coarse sea salt ground in a special mill is preferred to refined, free-running salt, especially for use at the table. Cooking salt can be used in the kitchen.

Vanilla *(vaniolia)*: pods are used to give flavour to sweet dishes, particularly custards. Vanilla essences and flavouring are used less often. Although expensive to buy, vanilla pods can be dried after use and then used again and again. Vanilla sugar is a popular ingredient in baking, and is available in sachets at Italian delicatessens, but it will taste better if made at home by simply immersing a vanilla pod in an airtight container of caster sugar.

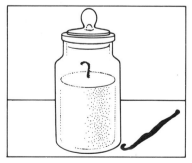

Vanilla pod in sugar

OTHER FLAVOURING INGREDIENTS

Capers *(capperi)*: these little green shrivelled buds are used whole and crushed in many Italian dishes, but particularly in fish dishes, sauces and stuffings. Always sold pickled in brine, they should be used sparingly as their flavour is very pungent.

Garlic *(aglio)*: while not all Italian food is heavily laced with garlic, although it seems to have earned this reputation abroad — mainly because most Italian

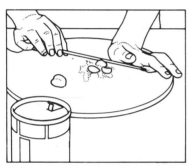

Crushing garlic with salt

emigrés come from southern Italy where garlic is very popular, especially in sauces to serve with pasta. Certain classic dishes rely heavily on its flavour, such as the Genoese pesto sauce, but otherwise garlic is used sparingly. Adjust quantities in recipes to suit your own taste, and crush the flesh with salt to help aid digestion.

Pine nuts *(pinoli)*: popular in all parts of the Mediteranean, the Italians love these tiny, white elongated nuts for their unique, delicate flavour and creamy texture. They are used in sauces (they are a classic ingredient in pesto), stuffings and sprinkled over vegetables; they are also used in sweet dishes.

Olive *(olive)* and **olive oil** *(olio d'olive)*: both black and green olives are extremely popular, eaten on their own with aperitifs or as part of antipasto, and in cooking.

The best Italian olives are sold loose in delicatessens; these are plump and juicy, sometimes pitted, and tossed in herbs and oil. Italian olive oil rates as one of the best in the world, and there are literally hundreds of different brands to choose from. Always buy the best quality, virgin olive oil *(olio extra vergine d'olive)* which is made from the first cold

Olive oil

pressing of the olives. Although expensive, this oil is thick in consistency, with a good, rich green colour. Refined oils from later hot pressings are pale and thin in comparison. Always use olive oil for salads and other cold dishes, but for cooking Italian dishes where a lighter flavour is preferred, you can use a vegetable or sunflower oil, or a mixture.

PREPARATION OF INGREDIENTS

There are very few difficult techniques in Italian cookery, but less familiar ingredients need specialist treatment. The Italian cook is well used to dealing with ingredients such as squid and mussels, because these are widely available in Italy—and used frequently. The steps and illustrations which follow will help you when dealing with these ingredients.

FRESH SQUID (CALAMARE)

Fresh squid is available at high-class fishmongers; it is not a seasonal fish, but if you require it for a specific recipe it is best to check with your fishmonger in advance regarding its availability. If not in stock, he may be able to order it for you from the market.

Some fishmongers will prepare squid for you free of charge, but it is as well to know how to do this yourself. Don't be put off by its unsightly appearance when raw, it is quick and simple to prepare provided you follow the steps closely. The end result is so good you will be rewarded for taking the time and trouble over its preparation.

When choosing fresh squid, look for flesh that is firm to the touch. The tentacles and body pouch are used in cooking and the rest is discarded (see steps on opposite page). Cuttlefish and octopus are prepared in a similar way and may be substituted for squid in some recipes. However, it should be remembered that octopus needs long, slow cooking in order to tenderise the firmer, thicker flesh.

The Italians use squid in seafood salads (see page 24) and fish soups, and in main course fish stews; they are also very fond of it coated in batter and deep-fried then served hot with lemon wedges. With a fresh green salad, this makes a delicious lunch dish.

TO CLEAN FRESH SQUID

1 Hold the squid under cold running water to rinse thoroughly. Pull back the edge of the body pouch to expose the translucent quill or pen.

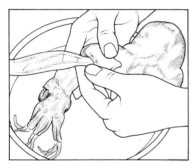

2 Holding the body pouch firmly with one hand, take hold of the end of the exposed quill with the other and pull it free. Then discard the quill.

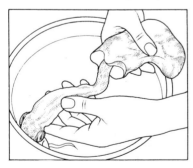

3 Separate the head and tentacles from the body pouch. Holding the body pouch in one hand, pull out the head and tentacles with the other.

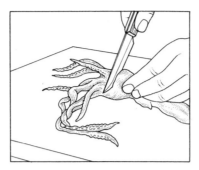

4 Cut through the head, just above the eyes. Discard the eyes and ink sac and reserve the tentacles. Wash them under cold running water, rubbing off the purplish skin.

5 Cut the tentacles into small pieces. If they are very small, leave some whole.

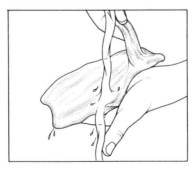

6 Rub the purplish skin off the body pouch, holding it under cold running water. Discard skin.

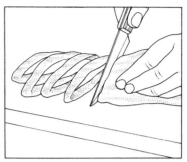

7 Using a sharp knife, carefully cut the triangular fins off the body pouch. Discard the fins and cut the body into thin rings.

FRESH MUSSELS
(COZZE)

The flavour of fresh mussels cannot possibly be compared with that of canned or bottled mussels, which are usually preserved in brine.

Fresh mussels have a unique soft texture and flavour of the sea, especially if they are freshly caught. They are easy to obtain at fishmongers at most times of year; frozen shelled mussels are also often available, at freezer centres and large supermarkets as well as fishmongers.

Always buy fresh mussels on the day you intend to eat them. You should deal with them as soon as you can after getting home, but if this is not possible, put them to soak in a large bowl of cold water until you are ready. Swirl in 15 ml (1 tbsp) fine oatmeal if you have it to hand—this passes through the intestines of the mussels and 'flushes them out' prior to pre-paration. Discard the water and rinse the mussels when you are ready to deal with them.

Italians use fresh mussels in an enormous number of different ways, but they are especially fond of them with the flavour of garlic. Stuffed cold mussels are a favourite antipasto, and mussels are almost always included in fish salads, soups and stews.

TO PREPARE FRESH MUSSELS

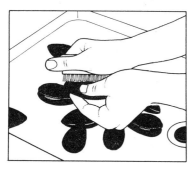

1 Put the mussels in a sink and scrub them with a hard brush in several changes of water.

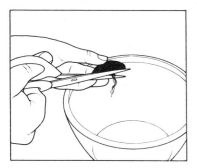

2 Scrape off any barnacles with a sharp knife. Then, with a pair of scissors, cut off any beards, or tufts of hair, which may protrude from the shell.

3 Leave mussels to soak in a bowl of cold water for 20 minutes, then discard any that are not tightly closed or do not close on giving them a sharp tap. This is an important part of the preparations process—any mussel that remains open is not alive and should not be cooked.

TO COOK FRESH MUSSELS

4 Put the mussels in a large saucepan. Pour in a few table-spoons of white wine or water. Add 1–2 chopped garlic cloves, a few sprigs of fresh parsley and seasoning to taste.

5 Cover the pan with a tight-fitting lid and bring to the boil. Cook for 5–10 minutes over high heat until the shells open, shaking the pan frequently.

6 Serve the mussels whole or on the half shell for a starter in individual soup bowls, with fresh bread to 'mop up' the cooking liquor. Alternatively, drain and use in individual recipes, reserving the cooking liquor if required.

DRINKS

WINES

Most wines are for immediate enjoyment rather than long keeping, and it is rare that you will find a truly 'great' wine outside Italy. Look for Denominazione di Origine Controllata (DOC) on wine labels, which is the equivalent to the French Appellation Contrôlée, the best sign of quality if you are unsure of a wine you have not tried before. Denominazione di Origine Controllata e Garantita (DOCG) denotes a really top-quality wine which must bear a government seal.

RED WINES

Barbaresco: from Piedmont, a prolific wine-producing area. Made from the Nebbiolo grape, and said to be one of Italy's best red wines. A fairly delicate-tasting wine, which is good when drunk young, with red meats.

Barbera: from Piedmont, made from the Barbera grape. Ruby-red, with a fruity bouquet. Look also for *Barbera d'Asti*, which is said to be the best. Both are all-purpose red wines, but are especially good with strong-tasting dishes.

Bardolino: from the region of Veneto, one of Italy's best-liked wines. Light and moderately fruity, it is good when drunk young and cool.

Barolo: from Piedmont's Nebbiola grape. One of Italy's best wines, sometimes described as 'the Burgundy of Italy'. With a robust, full flavour, it is perfectly suited to game.

Brunello di Montalcino: the most expensive of Italian wines. From the Tuscan Sangiovese grape, this wine is ruby-red, dry and full-flavoured. Matured in wood for at least 4 years before it is sold, a special occasion wine to serve with game and red meats.

Cabernet: Italian versions of this Bordeaux wine are made in the north-east of Italy and are well worth trying. Serve with red meats.

Chianti: the best known of all Italian red wines, from Tuscany. Young non-vintage chianti comes in litre flasks; fruity and fragrant, it goes well with light dishes. Vintage chiantis are fine, full-bodied wines—*Chianti Classico* is the name to look for, also *Chianti Vecchio* and *Chianti Riserva*, all excellent wines for serving with poultry and steaks.

Lambrusco: from the Po valley in Emilia-Romagna. Varies from very dry to sweet, but always slightly sparkling. It is light, pleasant wine, best served chilled.

Merlot: like Cabernet, an Italian wine made from a Bordeaux grape. Good with red meats.

Pinot: from the north-east, made from the French Pinot Noir grape. Look for the lively *Pinot Nero dell' Alto Adige*, suitable for any main course dish.

Valpolicella: a famous wine from the Veneto region. Smooth and light, with a sweet bouquet. A very 'drinkable' table wine which goes particularly well with pasta, veal and poultry. Look for *Recioto Amarone della Valpolicella* (called *Amarone*), a full-bodied wine for special occasions.

WHITE WINES
Asti Spumante: the world-famous sparkling white, which is made in Piedmont from the Muscat grape and exported from there in vast quantities. Dry Astis are sold, but the sweet, fruity varieties with a pronounced bouquet are more common. Drink well chilled. as an aperitif or dessert wine.

Est! Est! Est!: a not altogether reliable wine, but famous nevertheless—most probably because of its unusual name. The best variety comes from Montefiascone. A dry, fresh-tasting wine which goes well with fish.

Frascati: a well-known wine from the town of the same name near Rome—one of the 'castelli romani' wines from the hills south-east of the capital. A fruity, dry wine, the best are drunk young and chilled. Look also for sweet Frascati, called *Canellino*, with its wonderful bouquet and bronze-gold colour: an excellent dessert wine.

Lacrima Christi: from the Bay of Naples. There are dry and sweet versions, all having the same slight 'mineral' taste from the volcanic soil of Mt Vesuvius.

Orvieto: from the town of the same name in Umbria. Dry Orvieto *(secco)* is the most popular table wine, but there is also a semi-dry version *(abbocato)* and a semi-sweet *(amabile)*. Orvieto is sold in the same traditional wicker-covered flask as Chianti, but is smaller in size. Serve chilled, with fish or white meat dishes.

Pinot Bianco and Pinot Grigio: both from the north, made from the classic wine grape. Fruity, fresh and dry, these wines are good value and worth trying.

Soave: a famous wine from Veneto. Fragrant and fruity, yet dry and light—an excellent accompaniment to virtually any type of dish.

Verdicchio: from central Italy, this very dry white wine has a unique curved bottle like a Roman amphora. Best described as crisp, it goes well with bland dishes.

Vernaccia: a Sardinian wine, which can be dry or sweet. Dry Vernaccia is excellent with fish and shellfish.

DIGESTIFS, FORTIFIED WINES AND LIQUEURS
Amaretto: a liqueur made from apricot kernels, with a strong almond flavour. Most often served straight as an after-dinner drink, but also drunk with ice as an aperitif. Useful also for dessert recipes, especially with peaches.

Aurum: an unusual brandy-based liqueur, which is not widely available, but worth seeking out for its sharp, tangy flavour of oranges and herbs. To be drunk as a digestif after dinner.

Fernet and Fernet Branca: strong-tasting digestifs or 'bitters' made from herbs in Turin and Milan respectively.

Galliano: a herb-based liqueur from Lombardy in a tall, tapering bottle. It is golden-yellow in colour and syrupy sweet, with a hint of vanilla about its flavour. Often used in cocktails.

Grappa: equivalent to the French marc; a spirit made from the leftovers (skin, pips, stalks) of grapes after the final pressing in wine making. Colourless and deceptively strong, it is extremely fiery when young, but mellows slightly with age.

Maraschino: a liqueur or cherry brandy. Drink as an after-dinner liqueur or use in desserts.

Marsala: a fortified wine. Dry Marsala makes an unusual aperitif, whereas sweet Marsala is drunk as a dessert wine. *Marsala all' uovo* is made with egg yolks and is a traditional ingredient in the dessert zabaglione. Italians often use Marsala in cooking—its slightly roasted or 'burnt' flavour is good with veal and desserts.

Strega: a yellow liqueur with a strong flavour of herbs, sweet and strong. Used a lot in cocktails and desserts, especially ice cream.

Basic Recipes

In this chapter you will find all the basic recipes you need to help you with the Italian recipes in the colour section of this book. How to make your own pasta (with cooking and serving instructions and quantities) and homemade pizza dough (both yeast and scone dough methods). Plus a whole section of sauces, dressings and stocks.

SAUCES TO SERVE WITH PASTA

The choice of sauces to serve with pasta is almost limitless, and every region has its own specialities depending on the local produce grown. For example, pesto sauce made with a large quantity of basil comes from Liguria where basil grows so prolifically, and most of the tomato sauces originate from the Naples area where tomatoes are at their best. Some pasta sauces are hot, others cold—the heat of the freshly cooked pasta warms them through by the time they are served. The following recipes are just a small selection of the best-known and best-liked sauces to serve with pasta. Information on making, cooking and serving pasta is on pages 150–151. Equipment for making pasta is on pages 152–153.

SALSA DI POMODORO CRUDO
(Uncooked Tomato Sauce)
Makes enough to dress 4 servings of pasta

| 350 g (12 oz) tomatoes, skinned and seeded |
| 1 garlic clove, skinned and finely chopped |
| 75 ml (5 tbsp) olive oil |
| 1 basil or parsley sprig, chopped |
| salt and freshly ground pepper |

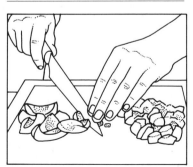

1 Chop the tomatoes roughly and place in a bowl.

2 Add the remaining ingredients and stir well to mix. Cover and leave to marinate for at least 6 hours. Stir well and taste and then adjust seasoning before serving cold with freshly cooked pasta.

SALSA DI POMODORO
(Simple Tomato Sauce)
Makes enough to dress 4 servings of pasta

| 450 g (1 lb) tomatoes, skinned and roughly chopped, or 397 g (14 oz) can tomatoes, with their juice |
| 1 small onion, skinned and roughly chopped |
| 1 garlic clove, skinned and chopped |
| 1 celery stick, sliced |
| 1 bay leaf |
| sprig of parsley |
| 2.5 ml ($\frac{1}{2}$ tsp) sugar |
| salt and freshly ground pepper |

1 Place all the ingredients in a saucepan, bring to the boil then simmer, uncovered, for 30 minutes until thickened. Stir occasionally to prevent sticking to the bottom of the pan.

2 Remove the bay leaf and purée the mixture in an electric blender or food processor until smooth or push through a sieve using a wooden spoon. Reheat and then taste and adjust seasoning. Serve the sauce hot with freshly cooked pasta.

SALSA DI POMODORO ALLA NAPOLETANA
(Neapolitan Tomato Sauce)

Makes enough to dress 4 servings of pasta

700 g (1½ lb) tomatoes, skinned and roughly chopped, or a 397 g (14 oz) and a 226 g (8 oz) can tomatoes, with their juice

1 garlic clove, skinned and crushed

75 ml (5 tbsp) olive oil

1 sprig of fresh oregano, marjoram, basil or parsley, or 2.5 ml (½ tsp) dried

2.5 ml (½ tsp) sugar

salt and freshly ground pepper

1 Place all the ingredients in a large saucepan and bring to the boil.

2 Lower the heat and simmer, uncovered, for about 10 minutes until the oil has separated from the tomatoes. Stir frequently.

3 Taste and adjust seasoning before serving hot, with freshly cooked pasta.

RAGÙ *(Bolognese Sauce)*

Makes enough to dress 4 servings of pasta

30 ml (2 tbsp) olive oil

25 g (1 oz) butter

2 rashers of pancetta or smoked streaky bacon, rinded and finely chopped

1 small onion, skinned and finely chopped

225 g (8 oz) minced beef

1 garlic clove, skinned and finely chopped

1 small celery stick, finely chopped

1 small carrot, peeled and finely chopped

1 bay leaf

30 ml (2 tbsp) tomato purée

150 ml (¼ pint) dry white wine

150 ml (¼ pint) beef stock

salt and freshly ground pepper

1 Heat the oil and butter in a saucepan and fry the pancetta or bacon and chopped onion for 2–3 minutes until soft.

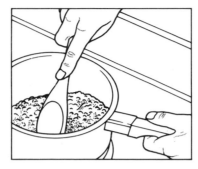

2 Add the minced beef and cook for a further 5 minutes, stirring constantly to break up any lumps, until it is lightly browned.

3 Add the garlic, celery, carrot and bay leaf and cook, stirring, for a further 2 minutes.

4 Stir in the tomato purée, wine, stock and seasoning. Bring to the boil, then lower the heat, cover and simmer for 1–1½ hours, stirring occasionally. Discard the bay leaf.

5 Taste and adjust seasoning before serving hot, with freshly cooked pasta.

SALSA DI PANNA
(Cream Sauce)

Makes enough to dress 4 servings of pasta

25 g (1 oz) butter

300 ml (10 fl oz) double cream

25 g (1 oz) freshly grated Parmesan cheese, plus extra for serving

salt and freshly ground pepper

1 Melt the butter in a saucepan, pour in the cream and bring to the boil. Cook for 2–3 minutes, stirring constantly, until slightly thickened. Stir in the Parmesan cheese with seasoning to taste.

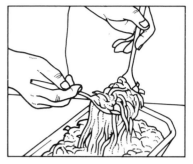

2 Pour over freshly cooked pasta and toss together before serving, with extra cheese handed separately.

SALSA DI TONNO
(Tuna Fish Sauce)

Makes enough to dress 4 servings of pasta

200 g (7 oz) can tuna, drained and flaked

226 g (8 oz) can tomatoes, with their juice

15 ml (1 tbsp) chopped fresh parsley

salt and freshly ground pepper

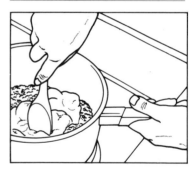

1 Place all the ingredients in a saucepan. Break up the tomatoes with a wooden spoon and then bring to the boil, stirring.

2 Lower the heat and simmer, uncovered, for 5 minutes or until hot. Taste and adjust seasoning.

3 Pour over freshly cooked pasta, and toss together before serving.

AJO E OJO
(Garlic and Oil Sauce)

Makes enough to dress 4 servings of pasta

120 ml (8 tbsp) olive oil

2 garlic cloves, skinned and finely chopped

salt and freshly ground pepper

1 Place the oil, garlic and seasoning in a small saucepan and fry very gently, stirring all the time, for 2–3 minutes until the garlic is golden brown.

2 Pour over freshly cooked pasta, and toss together before serving.

PESTO
(Basil and Pine Nut Sauce)

This sauce can be stored for up to 2 weeks in a screw-topped jar in the refrigerator.

Makes enough to dress 4 servings of pasta

50 g (2 oz) fresh basil leaves

2 garlic cloves, skinned

30 ml (2 tbsp) pine nuts

salt and freshly ground pepper

100 ml (4 fl oz) olive oil

50 g (2 oz) Parmesan cheese

1 Place the basil, garlic, pine nuts, seasoning and olive oil in an electric blender or food processor and blend until very creamy.

2 Transfer the mixture to a bowl, grate in the cheese and then mix together thoroughly. Taste and adjust seasoning before serving.

SAUCES AND DRESSING FOR SALADS

Simple dressings of olive oil, lemon juice and seasoning are popular in Italy with plain green and mixed salads, and fresh herbs are used to give extra flavour.

SALSA DI NOCI
(Walnut Dressing)

This sauce can be stored for up to 1 week in a screw-topped jar in the refrigerator.

Makes 225 ml (8 fl oz)

1 small slice wholemeal bread

40 g (1½ oz) walnuts

10 ml (2 tsp) lemon juice

1 garlic clove, skinned

salt and freshly ground pepper

200 ml (7 fl oz) olive oil

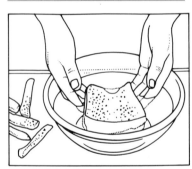

1 Remove the crusts from the slice of bread and soak it in cold water for a few minutes.

2 Squeeze out the excess moisture and place the bread in a food processor.

3 Add the walnuts, lemon juice, garlic and seasoning and blend until the mixture is very finely ground.

4 Gradually add the oil through the funnel, while the machine is still running, until it is all incorporated. Check the seasoning and stir well before use.

SALSA VERDE
(Green Sauce)

This sauce can be stored for 2–3 weeks in a screw-topped jar in the refrigerator.

Makes enough to dress 4 servings of fish or boiled meat

100 ml (4 fl oz) olive oil

15 ml (1 tbsp) white wine vinegar or lemon juice

45 ml (3 tbsp) chopped fresh parsley

30 ml (2 tbsp) capers, chopped

1 garlic clove, skinned and finely chopped

3 anchovy fillets, finely chopped

2.5 ml (½ tsp) prepared mustard

freshly ground pepper

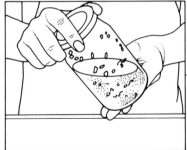

Place all the ingredients in a bowl or screw-topped jar and whisk or shake together.

SALSA PER INSALATA
(Salad Dressing)
This sauce can be stored for 2–3 weeks in a screw-topped jar in the refrigerator.

Makes 150 ml ($\frac{1}{4}$ pint)

120 ml (8 tbsp) olive oil

30 ml (2 tbsp) lemon juice

1 garlic clove, skinned and crushed

2 anchovy fillets, crushed

freshly ground pepper

Place all the ingredients in a bowl or screw-topped jar and whisk or shake together.

MAKING MAYONNAISE
Making mayonnaise is not difficult, but many cooks are daunted by the prospect of it curdling. Once you have mastered the art, you will find its flavour and thick, velvety smooth texture far superior to any kind of commercial mayonnaise. If you follow the recipe exactly, and observe the following few guide-lines, you are unlikely to have problems with curdling.

1 Always use top-quality ingredients. Italian olive oil is thick and rich, ideal for making mayonnaise. Look for brands from Lucca, which are said to be some of the best in Italy. Olive oil gives a dark, flavoursome mayonnaise; if you prefer a lighter result, then mix the olive oil with some vege-table or corn oil (half and half is a good ratio)—this will also turn out to be less expensive than using all olive oil.

Use wine vinegar or lemon juice, *not* malt vinegar, for the acid ingredient required in mayonnaise to thin down the oil and egg emulsion. Malt vinegar is far too strong in flavour.

2 Remember the ratio of oil to eggs: 150 ml ($\frac{1}{4}$ pint) oil to every egg yolk. If you prefer a lighter result, then you can use a whole egg, in which case you will need 300 ml ($\frac{1}{2}$ pint) oil.

3 All ingredients must be at room temperature. Eggs taken straight from the refrigerator and oil from a cold larder are almost guaranteed to end in curdling. Sometimes the mixing bowl is too cold—a wise precaution is to warm it before starting.

4 When starting to make the mayonnaise, after you have mixed the egg with the seasoning, add the oil *a drop at a time* and beat vigorously until the mixture begins to thicken or emulsify. This is the stage where most cooks go wrong—by trying to hurry the addition of the oil. If the oil and egg do not emulsify at this stage the mayonnaise will curdle.

5 Once the egg and oil have emulsified, add the remaining oil in a *thin, steady stream*. Again, do not hurry this step, or the oil will form a separate layer. Add the oil gradually and beat vigorously all the time. If you find the mixture is becoming too thick to add more oil, then thin it down with some of the vinegar or lemon juice (the rest should be beaten in at the end).

6 If the mayonnaise curdles while you are making it, it can be rescued in several ways. Put a fresh egg yolk into a clean bowl and then gradually incorporate the curdled mixture, beating hard. Once the mixture is smooth, you can then continue adding more oil. As an alternative to starting with a fresh egg yolk, you can also use 5 ml (1 tsp) hot water, wine vinegar, lemon juice or Dijon mustard.

MAIONESE *(Mayonnaise)*
Can be stored for 2–3 weeks in a screw-topped glass jar in the refrigerator.

Makes 150 ml ($\frac{1}{4}$ pint)

1 egg yolk

2.5 ml ($\frac{1}{2}$ tsp) mustard powder or 5 ml (1 tsp) prepared mustard

salt and freshly ground pepper

2.5 ml ($\frac{1}{2}$ tsp) sugar

15 ml (1 tbsp) lemon juice

about 150 ml ($\frac{1}{4}$ pint) mixture of olive oil and sunflower oil

1 Put the egg yolk in a bowl with the mustard, seasoning, sugar and 5 ml (1 tsp) of the lemon juice. Mix thoroughly.

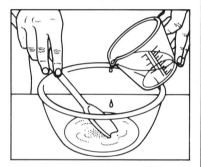

2 Add the oil, drop by drop, stirring briskly with a wooden spoon the whole time, or whisking constantly, until thick and smooth.

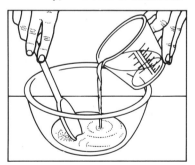

3 Continue adding the oil in a thin, steady stream, beating vigorously all the time.

4 If it becomes too thick, add a little more lemon juice. When all the oil has been added, mix in the remaining lemon juice. Adjust seasoning before serving.

BÉCHAMEL SAUCE

Béchamel is simply a white sauce made with infused milk, which gives it extra flavour. Here a bay leaf is used, but you can use peppercorns, bouquet garni and even a slice or two of raw onion.

BESCIAMELLA

(Béchamel Sauce)

Makes 300 ml ($\frac{1}{2}$ pint)

300 ml ($\frac{1}{2}$ pint) milk

1 bay leaf

25 g (1 oz) butter

25 g (1 oz) plain flour

pinch of grated nutmeg

salt and freshly ground pepper

1 Put the milk and bay leaf in a saucepan and slowly bring to the boil. Remove from the heat.

2 Melt the butter in a separate saucepan. Sprinkle in the flour and cook over low heat for 1–2 minutes, stirring with a wooden spoon. Do not allow the mixture (roux) to brown. Remove the pan from the heat.

3 Discard the bay leaf from the milk. Gradually blend the milk into the roux, stirring after each addition to prevent lumps forming.

4 Bring to the boil slowly and continue to cook, stirring all the time, until the sauce thickens.

5 Simmer very gently for a further 2–3 minutes. Add the nutmeg with seasoning to taste before serving.

STOCKS

Any dish which calls for chicken or beef stock will benefit from the full flavour of a homemade stock. This is particularly true of Italian sauces; stock cubes can of course be used, but the Italian cook always prefers to use homemade.

BEEF STOCK

Makes about 1.4 litres (2$\frac{1}{2}$ pints)

450 g (1 lb) marrowbone or knuckle of veal, chopped

450 g (1 lb) shin of beef, cut into pieces

1.7 litres (3 pints) water

bouquet garni

1 onion, skinned and sliced

1 carrot, peeled and sliced

1 celery stick, washed, trimmed and sliced

salt

1 To give a good flavour and colour, brown the bones and meat in the oven (exact temperature not important) before using.

2 Put the browned bones and meat in a large saucepan with the water, bouquet garni, vegetables and 2.5 ml ($\frac{1}{2}$ tsp) salt. Bring the liquid to the boil.

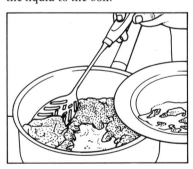

3 With a slotted spoon, skim off the scum and then simmer, covered, for 5–6 hours.

4 Strain the stock thoroughly, discarding the vegetables. Leave to cool. Remove the solidified fat before using.

CHICKEN STOCK

Makes 1.1–1.4 litres (2–2$\frac{1}{2}$ pints)

carcass and bones of a cooked chicken

1.4–1.7 litres (2$\frac{1}{2}$–3 pints) water

1 onion, skinned and sliced

1 carrot, peeled and sliced

1 celery stick, washed, trimmed and sliced

bouquet garni (optional)

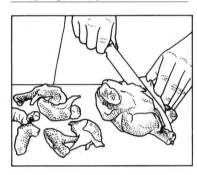

1 Break down the carcass and bones of the cooked chicken, and make sure to include any skin and chicken scraps.

2 Put in a pan with the water, onion, carrot, celery and the bouquet garni, if using.

3 Bring the liquid to the boil, skim off the scum with a slotted spoon and simmer, covered, for 3 hours.

4 Strain the stock thoroughly, discarding the flavouring vegetables, and leave to cool. When cold, remove all traces of fat.

MAKING PIZZAS

For pizzas made the way the Italians make them in pizzerias, you will need to make a yeast dough. This is similar to ordinary white bread and gives a soft, medium thick base. Special pizza pans are available for baking, which keep the dough in a neat, circular shape. If you do not have these, use ordinary sandwich tins or flan rings placed on a baking sheet. You can make pizzas straight on baking sheets, but they do tend to spread and become misshapen during rising and cooking, so it is best to use a container when you are making round pizzas.

On this page is a recipe using yeast for Basic Pizza Dough, which is sufficient to make one large rectangular pizza (about 37.5 × 30 cm/15 × 12 inches), two 27.5 cm (11 inch) pizzas, or four 20 cm (8 inch) pizzas. Toppings are in the chapter on pizzas on pages 52–61. If you do not have time to make a yeast dough, then a quicker base can be made from scone dough—see the recipe for Quick Pizza Dough below—which makes the same quantity. Alternatively, you can use packet white bread mix—you will need two 284 g (10 oz) packets. Oven temperatures and times are the same for all doughs.

BASIC PIZZA DOUGH

45 ml (3 tbsp) lukewarm milk
20 g (¾ oz) fresh yeast
3.75 ml (¾ tsp) sugar
300 g (11 oz) strong white bread flour
7.5 ml (1½ tsp) salt
30 ml (2 tbsp) olive oil
about 90 ml (6 tbsp) lukewarm water

1 Put the milk in a warmed jug and crumble in the yeast with your fingers. Add the sugar and stir to dissolve, then stir in 4 tbsp of the flour.

2 Cover the jug with a clean tea towel and leave in a warm place for about 30 minutes or until frothy.

3 Sift the remaining flour and the salt into a warmed large bowl. Mix in the yeast with a fork, then add the oil and enough water to draw the mixture together.

4 Turn the dough out on to a floured surface and knead for 10 minutes until it is smooth and elastic.

5 Put the ball of dough in a large floured bowl, cover with a clean tea towel and leave in a warm place for 1½–2 hours until doubled in bulk.

QUICK PIZZA DOUGH

450 g (1 lb) self-raising flour
5 ml (1 tsp) salt
100 g (4 oz) butter or margarine
300 ml (½ pint) milk

1 Sift the flour and salt into a bowl, then rub in the butter until the mixture resembles fine breadcrumbs.

2 Add the milk and mix to a soft dough. Turn out onto a lightly floured work surface and knead until smooth. Roll out the dough and cut into shapes as required.

THE ORIGIN OF THE PIZZA

The original pizza was invented by bakers as a means of using up leftover pieces of dough at the end of bread-making. It originated in one of the poorer parts of southern Italy, in and around the city of Naples, where food was never that plentiful that it could afford to be wasted.

The original pizzas were very plain, with a simple topping of tomatoes and cheese, but nowadays Pizza Napoletana often has anchovies and black olives included in its topping. This pizza is perhaps the best known outside Italy because it was initially the Neapolitans who emigrated to the United States of America and Great Britain where they opened up the first pizza houses or *pizzerie*. Nowadays there are literally hundreds of different toppings for pizza, but Pizza Napoletana stays a favourite.

You may wonder why pizzas baked in *pizzerie* always have such a good, light dough, whether thin and crispy or thick and traditional. The reason for this is the oven, which reaches an exceptionally high temperature—essential for 'setting' the dough. Domestic ovens produce a very good result, but obviously cannot reach this same high temperature.

MAKING PASTA AT HOME

You will find making pasta at home very easy—the actual dough is a simple mixture of just four ingredients—flour, salt, eggs and olive oil. Both the flavour and texture of homemade pasta are far superior to any dried pasta, and even better than the so-called 'fresh pasta' that is now widely available in supermarkets and delicatessens. Even in composite dishes such as lasagne, you will find fresh pasta tastes better and gives a much lighter result. Follow these step-by-step instructions and illustrations and you simply can't go wrong, even if you're a complete novice.

The best flour to use is semolina flour: a hard, very fine wheat flour. As this is difficult to obtain, a strong flour of the type used in breadmaking is a satisfactory alternative. General household plain flour can be used, but it produces a dough which cannot be rolled out as thinly by hand—it is best to use this only if you have a pasta machine (see page 152) for rolling and cutting the dough. Eggs which have deep yellow yolks are preferred by Italian cooks to give a good, strong colour to the finished pasta. Free-range or farm fresh eggs should have the deepest yellow yolks, but it is not essential to use them.

BASIC EGG PASTA

300 g (11 oz) strong plain flour
5 ml (1 tsp) salt
3 eggs, size 2, beaten
15 ml (3 tsp) olive oil
water, if necessary

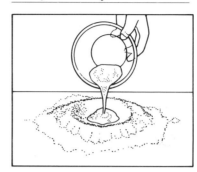

1 Sift the flour and salt into a mound on a working surface. Make a well in the centre, pour in the beaten eggs and olive oil.

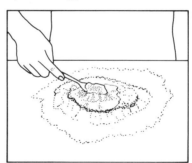

2 Start beating in the eggs with a fork, drawing in the flour gradually from around the well.

3 When the egg is no longer liquid, mix in the rest of the flour with the fingertips, working quickly.

4 If there are any dry areas, add a few drops of water to moisten them. Don't overwet the dough—it should look rough and lumpy at this stage. If you add too much water, the finished pasta will be tough and unpalatable.

5 Put the dough on to a clean, freshly floured surface. Flour your hands.

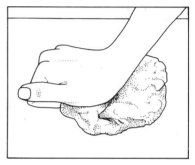

6 Knead the dough energetically as when you are making bread. Use the heel of the hand not the palm, folding the dough over towards you and pressing away each time.

7 Continue kneading for 10–15 minutes, at the end of which time the dough should be smooth and pliable—with little bubbles forming over the surface. (Do not skimp on the kneading time as this makes the dough elastic and easier to roll, especially essential if you are not using a pasta machine for rolling and cutting.)

8 Shape the dough into a ball and leave to rest for 10–20 minutes in a lightly floured bowl covered with a clean tea towel.

SHAPING THE DOUGH

This is the most difficult part of making pasta at home by hand; if you intend to make pasta regularly it is best to invest in a machine (see page 152). Rolling out the dough by hand is hard work and difficult to get really paper thin. For best results, work in a cool kitchen, use a good rolling pin (see page 152) and exercise a little patience!

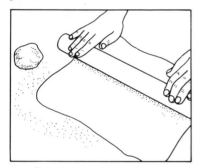

1 Place the ball of dough on a floured surface and roll out to a large rectangle which is nearly paper thin.

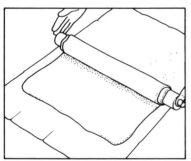

2 Carefully transfer the sheet of dough to a clean tea towel which has been previously sprinkled with flour. Leave to rest for about 1 hour, depending on the temperature and humidity of the room. Do not allow the pasta to dry out too much and become leathery or it will not cut properly.

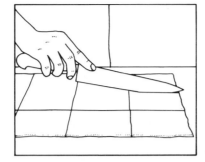

3 Cut the sheet of dough into the required shapes, using a sharp knife for lasagne and tagliatelle. (If you have a pasta or pastry wheel (see page 153), this will give a neater, more professional finish. For ravioli, you will need to use special equipment (see page 153).

4 After cutting, spread the pasta out on a floured clean tea towel and sprinkle with flour. Use within 24 hours.

COOKING AND SERVING PASTA

Pasta—both fresh and dried—is simplicity itself to cook, but there are a few do's and don'ts.

Don't overcook. Manufacturers of dried pasta give instructions on packets, but these are often over-long, and with fresh homemade pasta there are no instructions to follow. Italians judge the cooking time of their pasta by tasting it until it is 'al dente', that is, only just tender, but still with a slight resistance or 'bite' to it.

Do use as much water as possible. This is very important as it allows the pasta to swell. Too little water will cause pasta to clog together in a solid mass. The addition of oil to the cooking water helps prevent this problem.

Do drain the pasta thoroughly before serving, but *don't* mix it with the sauce. Italians pile the pasta in a warmed serving dish and pour the sauce over the top. The pasta and sauce are then tossed together at the time of serving. Freshly grated Parmesan cheese is handed separately.

TO COOK PASTA

4 litres (7 pints) water
45 ml (3 tbsp) salt
15 ml (1 tbsp) vegetable oil

1 In a very large saucepan, bring the water to the boil. Add the salt and swirl in the oil.

2 When the water is boiling very rapidly, drop in the pasta all at once. (This quantity of water is sufficient to cook 300–400 g (11–14 oz) fresh or dried pasta—do not attempt to cook more than this at one time or the pasta will stick.) Turn up the heat and quickly return the water to the boil. Calculate the cooking time from this moment, according to the following cooking times:
Unfilled pasta
Fresh: 2–3 minutes
Dried: 8–12 minutes
Filled pasta
Fresh: 8–10 minutes
Dried: 15–20 minutes

3 Drain the pasta in a colander immediately the cooking time is up. Allow time for all the water to drain thoroughly off the pasta, then pile into a warmed serving dish and toss with sauce, etc, according to individual recipes.

QUANTITIES OF PASTA

When calculating quantities of fresh or dried pasta per person, remember that they are exactly the same: fresh pasta is lighter in weight than dried, but it almost trebles in weight when cooked.

Italians always eat pasta as a course on its own, after the antipasto and before the main course. In Italy, 450 g (1 lb) pasta is usually served for 4–6 people, but if you are serving pasta as a starter before a substantial main course dish, then you will probably prefer to decrease this amount to 50–75 g (2–3 oz) per person. If you are serving pasta as a main course dish for an informal meal, then increase the quantity to 100 g–175 g (4–6 oz) per person.

Specialist Equipment

Italian cooking has very few complicated methods, and if you have a reasonably well-equipped kitchen, you will find you have most of the equipment needed to make any of the dishes in this book. There are certain specialised pieces of equipment to be found in Italian kitchens, however, and now most of these are available in specialist kitchen shops outside Italy—at very reasonable prices. If you and your family are fond of Italian food, it is well worth investing in a few of these items—to make preparation quicker and less painstaking. Listed on these pages are the most useful pieces of equipment, including a choice of *gelati*—delicious ice-cream recipes.

EQUIPMENT FOR MAKING PASTA

Pasta can be made successfully by hand, but when it comes to the rolling and cutting you will find it hard work—and quite difficult to get it really thin. You will also have to let the dough rest for up to an hour before cutting it, which, with such an unwieldy sheet of dough, you will find extremely inconvenient—especially if you are working in a small kitchen. A **pasta machine** allows you to roll and cut the dough in a matter of minutes, immediately after you have made it. It is simplicity itself to use, and the end result is always a beautifully smooth, even dough—with no hard work involved! Electric pasta machines imported from Italy are available at some specialist outlets; these will actually mix the dough and roll and cut it, but they are extremely expensive and only really

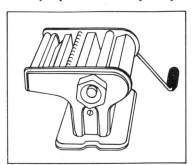
Hand-operated pasta machine

worth buying if you are frequently catering for large numbers. A much better buy is the hand-operated type of pasta machine (see illustration), which consists of three rollers. One roller is smooth for kneading and rolling the dough—it works in conjunction with a dial which you adjust to the required degree of thickness each time you put the dough through. The two other rollers have cutters, which you use according to the type of pasta you are making—

thick tagliatelle or thin tagliolini, for example. The rollers are turned by a handle, which requires very little in the way of effort, and the machine clamps on to the edge of the work surface to ensure stability. With some pasta machines, extra attachments can be bought separately for making spaghetti and ravioli. **Pasta making attachments** for free-

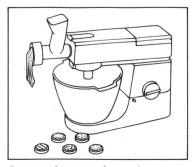
Pasta making attachment for mixer

standing large mixers are available, and are a good buy if you already have the mixer. They come with different screens for making different shapes such as lasagne, spaghetti, macaroni, etc.

If you do not have a pasta machine of any description, then you will need a good, heavy wooden **rolling pin** so that you can roll out the dough as thinly as

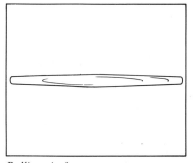
Rolling pin for pasta

possible. Modern pins with ball bearings are hopeless for pasta, the best kinds are those with tapered ends, made of sturdy beechwood for firm rolling out. A **pastry** or **pasta wheel** is a little gadget used for cutting out pasta. If you use an ordinary knife, this can sometimes

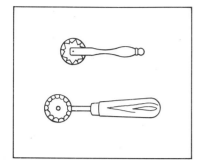

Pastry or pasta wheels

have the effect of dragging the pasta out of shape. A wheel does not do this, and is ideal for giving a neat, professional-looking edge to many different kinds of pasta, particularly lasagne and stuffed pasta shapes.

RAVIOLI

For making ravioli, which is extremely simple, there are various different pieces of equipment which will help give a more professional touch. A wooden **ravioli rolling pin** has sections

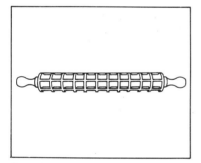

Ravioli rolling pin

or indentations which shape the squares of ravioli as you roll. Even better than this, however, is a **ravioli tray**, which usually has 36 squares and comes complete with a short beechwood rolling pin.

Ravioli tray and rolling pin

After rolling out the dough very thinly, it is placed over the tray, then pressed into each square with a small ball of left-over dough. The filling is then spooned into the squares, the dough brushed with beaten egg for sealing, and a second sheet or dough placed on top. When this top piece of dough is rolled over with the rolling pin, the individual squares are cut out. Another method of making ravioli is to use **individual ravioli cutters**. Made of metal,

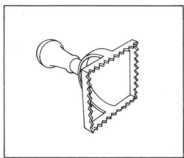

Ravioli cutter

with wooden handles, these can be shaped round or square. They make ravioli successfully—the filling is placed between two sheets of dough and then the cutter stamps out individual squares—but it is more time-consuming than using the tray and rolling pin method.

OTHER EQUIPMENT

Useful pieces of equipment for pasta making include a **spaghetti hook** or **rake**, which looks like a

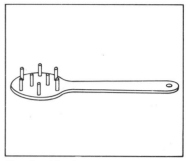

Spaghetti hook

flat wooden spoon with prongs attached. This is indispensable for removing spaghetti and other long pasta from the water and for serving, because the pasta does not slip off as it does with an ordinary spoon. Metal **spaghetti tongs**

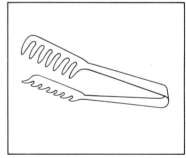

Spaghetti tongs

work in a similar way except that you have to grasp the strands of spaghetti in the tongs, which is slightly more tricky. Tongs with a spring action are the easiest to use.

Grated Parmesan cheese is served with many pasta dishes. Never use ready-grated Parmesan, the type that is sold in plastic tubs and sachets; this is dry and virtually tasteless, and hardly bears any resemblance to the real thing. Italians always buy their Parmesan cheese by the piece from a specialist cheese shop or delicatessen, and grate it freshly at home at the time when they need it (see page 135). The cheese is usually handed separately at the table in a special bowl with a small wooden spoon, but these Parmesan sets are difficult to obtain outside Italy.

Mature Parmesan cheese for grating is hard-textured and quite difficult to grate. Special **Parmesan knives** are available which are good for scraping off slivers or slices of cheese from a large piece.

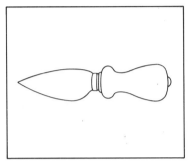

Parmesan knife

Metal **Parmesan graters** are also sold, and these grate the cheese to exactly the right degree of fineness required for serving with pasta.

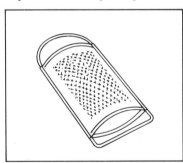

Parmesan grater

If you find it convenient to buy Parmesan in a large piece, the best way to deal with it is to cut it into smaller, more usable-sized pieces, then wrap each one individually in a double thickness of cling film or foil. Stored in the refrigerator it will keep its flavour for several weeks, in the freezer for at least 3 months. Remove individual packages as you need them.

(See page 150 for the basic pasta recipe, plus quantities, cooking and serving, and Pasta, Rice and Gnocchi (pages 31–51) for individual recipes.)

COFFEE MAKING MACHINES

The Italians love their coffee: large wide-brimmed cups of frothy white cappuccino in the morning, and tiny *demitasse* cups of strong, syrupy espresso after lunch or dinner. In Italian towns it seems almost every street corner has a coffee bar with the familiar steaming and hissing espresso machine, and Italians stop off for a coffee at any time of day or night. At home they also have domestic machines which produce a similar cup of coffee to the commercial ones.

Outside Italy, getting a good cup of cappuccino or espresso coffee is not so easy, apart from in an Italian restaurant or coffee shop. There are domestic espresso machines on the market, but these vary tremendously—some being more efficient than others. Many of them are so expensive that unless you happen to be an Italian coffee addict they are hardly worth the investment.

THE ESPRESSO METHOD

Making coffee by the espresso method is quite unique; entirely different from other methods such as filtering and percolating, for example, where the water simply passes over or through the coffee grounds. The espresso method works by *forcing* water through the coffee *under pressure*, and this is the essential difference. Espresso coffee is made instantly, and this is the secret behind its freshness and richness. Cappuccino is simply espresso coffee diluted with milk and foam, usually in the proportion of one third espresso to two-thirds milk.

TYPES OF COFFEE

The type of coffee is as important as the method of making it. The beans should be dark-roasted, sometimes called 'espresso roast', 'espresso blend', or even simply 'Italian' or 'continental'. The secret of freshness is to grind the beans *immediately* before you make the coffee, so buy whole beans in small amounts and grind them freshly every time. If you can buy beans from a specialist coffee shop which roasts on the premises, then so much the better. Roasting releases the essential oils in the beans which give the coffee its flavour. After roasting, evaporation begins and the beans start to lose flavour, so the sooner the coffee is made after roasting, the stronger the flavour. Freshly roasted beans will only keep their flavour (in a cool place) for 2 weeks at the most.

GRINDING THE COFFEE BEANS

An **electric coffee grinder** or **hand-operated coffee mill** is a

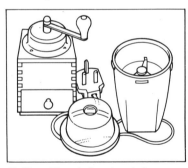

Coffee mill and electric grinder

must in the kitchen if you want the freshest possible coffee, and you must grind the beans as finely as possible—they should look gritty: be careful not to overgrind them to a powder. You can of course use an electric blender or food processor if you have one, but take great care to wash, rinse and dry it thoroughly after use. If you do not have a grinder of any description, then the coffee shop where you buy the beans will grind them for you—ask for 'very finely ground, suitable for use in an espresso machine'. Only buy in small amounts—ground coffee loses flavour and aroma much faster than beans and should never be kept longer than 1 week, even in an airtight container.

DIFFERENT TYPES OF ESPRESSO MACHINES

There are two basic types of espresso machine for domestic use. The most popular and least expensive is the **Moka Express,**

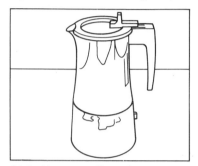

Moka Express coffee maker

the kind you use on top of the cooker. It is not quite so spectacular as the commercial and electric machines (see right), but if it is used properly, the end results are very good. There are many different types to choose from, some aluminium or stainless steel, others ceramic. Metal ones tend to impart a slight metallic taste to the coffee, so ceramic is probably the best choice. Different sizes are available, from as small as a 'two-cup', to as large as a 'twelve-cup'. These sizes tend to be on the conservative side, so it is best to buy a larger pot than you think you need. All these machines work on the same basic principle: fresh cold water is poured into the bottom container, coffee is packed firmly into the filter section, then the top section is screwed firmly on. After placing over medium heat for 5–6 minutes, the water boils and is forced up by steam pressure through the filter section into the top, which is then removed and used as a jug for serving.

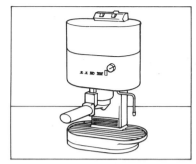

Electric espresso machine

Sophisticated **electric espresso machines,** looking rather like scaled-down versions of the commercial machines used in bars and restaurants, are now becoming increasingly widely available for home use. These machines have the advantage that they produce the frothy milk which is essential to make proper cappuccino, but they have distinct disadvantages. They are mostly extremely expensive and noisy—they are also quite complicated to use and a good deal of practice is required before you will be able to make perfect coffee every time. Worth persevering with if you want the real thing, however, and improvements are being made all the time. Prices should come down somewhat as more and more machines come on to the market.

ICE CREAM MAKERS

Ice cream became fashionable in Italy in the 19th century, and the craze has remained ever since. (Some say it was the Romans who invented it, others that the Arabs introduced it to the Italians in the 9th century, and yet others that Marco Polo brought the technique back from China!)

The ice cream parlour or gelateria is a popular meeting place for Italians, who can literally sit for hours over a drink and an ice cream or sorbet, relaxing, chatting and watching the world go by. Any visitor to Italy will be struck by the enormous choice of different flavours, colours and shapes in a gelateria, and at their tremendous popularity. Ice cream making at home is also popular, and there are various machines available to make the task easier.

Ice creams and sorbets made by hand never have quite the same velvety-smooth texture as those made by machine, for the simple reason that it is impossible to beat the mixture constantly as it freezes—and this is essential to stop large ice crystals forming and the texture of the ice cream being granular. Machine methods also give greater bulk from the same amount of mixture than hand-beating: about half as much again.

The original ice cream makers were **manually-operated churns,** and these are still avail-

Hand-operated ice cream churn

able at some specialist kitchen shops. The churn consists of a bucket, in the centre of which is a metal container to hold the ice cream mixture. The space around the container is packed with a mixture of ice and salt. A handle turns a dasher which churns the ice cream as it freezes. Churns are an extremely efficient method of making ice cream and the results are very good, but patience is needed and it is exhausting work turning the handle! **Electric churns** are now available, which work on the same principle as the hand-operated ones, and these are a much better buy.

An even less arduous way of making good ice cream is to use an **electric ice cream maker**. There are many different models on the market to choose from, some small and basic and relatively inexpensive, others elaborate pieces of expensive equipment that are quite suitable for professional use (and most of which are imported from Italy). Whatever the type, electric ice cream makers are altogether less involved than churns, which have to be packed with ice and salt (a messy job—even buying the ice can be a problem).

The basic **small type of ice cream maker or sorbetière**

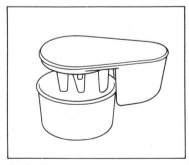

Sorbetière

works in the freezer or freezing compartment of the refrigerator turned to the coldest setting. (The flex is flat enough to go through the door of the freezer or refrigerator without interfering with the seal.) The ice cream or sorbet mixture is simply poured into the

machine, which is then placed in the freezer or freezing compartment and switched on. A small motor unit activates paddles which turn constantly through the mixture until it is smooth and thick, at which point they stop and/or lift up out of the mixture. Some machines have built-in fans which draw cold air into the mixture from the freezer; this makes freezing faster and the finished texture less grainy. After the paddles have finished working, the machine is left until the mixture is completely frozen and ready to serve. Nothing could be more simple or require less effort, and the end result is always a velvety-smooth ice cream or sorbet.

The more sophisticated and more expensive **ice cream makers**

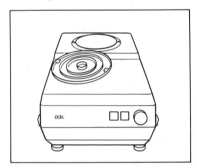

Free-standing ice cream maker

are the **electric free-standing types** that plug into a socket on the work surface. This type is fully automatic with its own built-in freezing unit, and so does not need to be placed in the freezer or refrigerator. The principle is the same as the more basic type, however, whereby a motor turns blades or paddles which churn through the mixture until it is the correct consistency; they then stop automatically and the mixture stays frozen in the machine until you are ready to serve. Overbeating is impossible with these machines, and they are well worth the expense if you intend to make ice creams or sorbets frequently— they can even be used for freezing yogurts, soups and drinks etc.

MAKING ICE CREAM (GELATO)

The Italians are justifiably famous for their ice creams—the number of different flavours is quite amazing. There are also numerous different ways of making gelato, some of which are only suitable for commercial machines. Our basic recipe is a simple one suitable for making at home; based on a rich egg custard mixture, it is full and creamy. Variations are suggested at the end of the recipe, but you can experiment by adding any ingredient or combination of ingredients you like.

Instructions are given for making the ice cream by hand, but if you have an ice cream maker, then so much the better—the finished texture will be smooth and creamy and you will have less work to do.

GUIDELINES TO SUCCESS WITH ICE CREAM MAKING

- Always use the exact amount of sugar specified in a recipe. Freezing reduces sweetness. Too much sugar will prevent the mixture from freezing properly; too little and the finished texture will be hard and rocky.
- Turn the refrigerator or freezer to its coldest setting before you start to make the ice cream. The quicker the mixture freezes, the smoother the texture will be (slow freezing produces large ice crystals in the mixture). Set the dial to coldest about 1 hour before you need to freeze the mixture, and don't forget to return the dial to its normal setting afterwards.

● If using the freezing compartment of the refrigerator, you will get a better texture if you stir the mixture every 30 minutes or so until it is at the half frozen or slushy stage (step 4 in the basic recipe). In a home freezer, this frequent stirring is not so necessary because the mixture freezes faster and there is therefore less chance of large ice crystals forming.

● Do not exceed the quantity of cream specified in a recipe. Too much cream gives an unpleasant grainy result.

SERVING ICE CREAM

● Let the ice cream 'come to' in the main body of the refrigerator before serving. This helps the flavour to mellow and makes the ice cream easier to both serve and eat.

Ice cream scoop

● If possible, use an ice cream scoop for serving. If not available, use a soup spoon and dip it in tepid water before making each scoop.

● Put scoops of ice cream in chilled individual glass dishes or stemmed glasses.

● Serve with wafers or crisp sweet biscuits. A cold fruit syrup or a hot sauce may be poured over the ice cream just before serving. Try to match the flavour of the sauce to that of the ice cream.

● Chopped nuts, crushed meringues or grated chocolate make a quick and easy topping which children will love.

GELATO *(Ice Cream)*

Serves 8–10

| 568 ml (1 pint) milk |
| 1 vanilla pod |
| 6 egg yolks |
| 175 g (6 oz) sugar |
| 568 ml (1 pint) whipping cream |

1 Bring the milk and vanilla pod almost to the boil. Take off the heat and leave to infuse for at least 15 minutes.

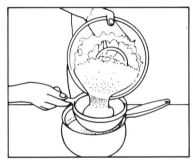

2 Beat the egg yolks and sugar together, stir in the milk and strain back into the pan.

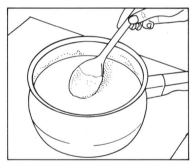

3 Cook the custard gently over a low heat, stirring until it coats the back of a wooden spoon. Do not boil.

4 Pour into a chilled, shallow freezer container and leave to cool. Then freeze the mixture for about 2 hours until slushy.

5 Turn the mixture into a large, chilled basin and mash with a flat whisk or fork.

6 Lightly whip the cream and fold into the mixture. Freeze again for about 2 hours until slushy, then mash again.

7 Return to the freezer for about 4 hours until firm. Allow to soften in the refrigerator for about 30 minutes before serving.

Note Do not whip the fresh cream if using a mechanical churn or electric ice cream maker. Agitate chilled custard and unwhipped cream together.

────── VARIATIONS ──────

Chocolate Break up 175 g (6 oz) plain chocolate, heat with the milk, whisking until smooth.
Coffee Stir 60 ml (4 tbsp) coffee and chicory essence into the made custard at the end of step 3.
Mango Peel 3 large mangoes and cut the flesh from the stone. Purée flesh in a blender or food processor and stir into made custard.
Peach Quarter 4 large peaches, remove the skin and stones. Purée the flesh in a blender or food processor and stir into made custard.
Strawberry Purée 350 g (12 oz) strawberries with 25 g (1 oz) icing sugar and 10 ml (2 tsp) lemon juice and stir into the made custard at the end of step 3.

TUTTI FRUTTI
(Fruit and Nut Ice Cream)

Serves 8

450 ml (¾ pint) milk

3 eggs

100 g (4 oz) caster sugar

300 ml (10 fl oz) double cream

150 ml (5 fl oz) single cream

100 g (4 oz) multi-coloured glacé cherries

50 g (2 oz) blanched almonds

50 g (2 oz) chopped mixed peel

1 Bring the milk to the boil then remove from the heat. Beat the eggs and sugar together until pale. Stir in the warm milk and strain back into the pan.

2 Stir the custard over a gentle heat until it coats the back of a wooden spoon. Do not boil. Leave to cool for about 30 minutes.

3 Whip the creams together and fold into the custard. Pour into a chilled, shallow freezer container and freeze for about 3 hours until slushy.

4 Meanwhile, halve the cherries and chop the almonds. Turn the frozen mixture into a large, chilled bowl and beat with a fork. Stir in the cherries, nuts and peel.

5 Return to the freezer container and freeze again for about 6 hours until firm. Transfer to the refrigerator to soften for 30 minutes before serving.

GELATO AL CIOCCOLATO, ALL' AVETA E AL RUM
(Chocolate, Raisin and Rum Ice Cream)

Serves 6

75 g (3 oz) raisins

45 ml (3 tbsp) dark rum

75 g (3 oz) plain chocolate

300 ml (½ pint) milk

2 eggs

50 g (2 oz) caster sugar

150 ml (5 fl oz) double cream

1 Finely chop the raisins and place in a large bowl. Pour over the rum and leave to stand while preparing the custard.

2 Break the chocolate into a heavy-based saucepan and add 60 ml (4 tbsp) milk. Heat gently until the chocolate has melted. Whisk in the remaining milk.

3 Beat the eggs and sugar together until pale. Pour in the chocolate milk then strain back into the pan.

4 Stir the custard over a gentle heat until it coats the back of a wooden spoon. Do not boil. Pour over the raisins, stir well and leave to cool for about 30 minutes.

5 Lightly whip the cream and fold into the custard. Pour into a chilled, shallow freezer container and freeze the mixture for about 3 hours until slushy and the ice cream is firm enough to support the weight of the raisins.

6 Turn the frozen mixture into a large, chilled bowl and beat with a fork, then stir to distribute the raisins evenly.

7 Return to the freezer container and freeze again for about 6 hours until firm. Transfer to the refrigerator to soften for 30 minutes before serving.

GELATO AL PISTACCHIO
(Pistachio Ice Cream)

Serves 4–6

300 ml (½ pint) milk

1 egg, plus 2 egg yolks

75 g (3 oz) caster sugar

green food colouring

300 ml (10 fl oz) double cream

50 g (2 oz) shelled pistachio nuts

1 Bring the milk to the boil then remove from the heat. Beat the egg, egg yolks and sugar together until pale. Stir in the warm milk and strain back into the pan.

2 Stir the custard over a gentle heat until it coats the back of a wooden spoon. Do not boil.

3 Pour into a large bowl and stir in a few drops of food colouring to tint pale green. Leave to cool for about 30 minutes.

4 Lightly whip the cream and fold into the custard. Pour into a chilled, shallow freezer container and freeze the mixture for about 3 hours until slushy.

5 Finely chop the nuts. Turn the frozen mixture into a large, chilled bowl and beat well with a fork. Stir in the nuts.

6 Return to the freezer container and freeze again for about 6 hours until firm. Transfer to the refrigerator to soften for 30 minutes before serving.

INDEX